BERTHOUD
from River Bottom *to* Bluff

MARK FRENCH

PUBLISHED BY

Slim Thompson Publications, LLC

To the historians of Berthoud:
William Turner, Ernest Newell, Belva Turner Bashor,
and Helen McCarty Fickel

Contents

continued

Part Two: Berthoud on the River Bottom

Part Three: Berthoud on the Bluff

          continued

Introduction

Unlike the Big Thompson River to the north and the St. Vrain River to the south, the Little Thompson was first and most accurately described as a creek. Each of the rivers roar to life in spring when snowfields in the Rocky Mountains melt and the icy water wends its way through foothill drainages to the plains. The Little Thompson gathers its water from the slopes of the Twin Sisters, located near the base of Longs Peak, the majestic "fourteener" that was named for explorer Stephen H. Long in 1820.

Mt. Meeker (center left), Longs Peak (center right) and the Twin Sisters (right), as seen from Berthoud, Colorado. (Mark French)

As the crow flies, the drainage of the Little Thompson extends 30 miles east from its source to its confluence with its sister river, the Big Thompson, near Milliken, Colorado. Dropping some 4,000 feet from its source to its last foothills' canyon, the valley of the Little Thompson broadens to a width of perhaps six or seven miles before it is absorbed into the larger drainages of the Big Thompson and eventually the South Platte River.

Berthoud—From River Bottom to Bluff is set in three adjoining townships that form an area roughly 20 miles long and five miles wide. The Little Thompson Valley spans the boundary of northern Boulder, southeast Larimer and western Weld counties and covers large expanses of Townships 4 North of Ranges 68, 69 and 70 West.

Divided into three parts, the book chronicles the history of the Little Thompson Valley from the dawn of the 1800s to the dusk of the 19th century.

The first part, **Before Berthoud**, provides a glimpse of the valley during the era of American Indians, fur trappers, explorers and early travelers on the Cherokee and Overland trails. The first settlers, primarily cattlemen who grazed their herds on the open range, are the principle characters.

Berthoud on the River Bottom, the second part, recounts the arrival of homesteaders including Lewis Cross, who helped the Little Thompson settlement spring to life in the early 1870s. Accounts of itinerant ministers, the formation of the valley's first school district, and the construction of the Colorado Central Railroad line establish the context for the relocation of the settlement, by then renamed Berthoud, during the winter of 1883-84.

Part Three, **Berthoud on the Bluff**, chronicles the growth of Berthoud and the surrounding Little Thompson Valley into the major agricultural center of southern Larimer County by the close of the 19th century (1899).

PART 1

BEFORE
BERTHOUD

Homesteading Chronology
of the Thompson Valley
— 1870s —

Note: This list does not include settlers who purchased land from the railroad.

1872
Cronk, George
Preffer, James

1873
Cross, Lewis

1874
Baxter, Davis
Bennett, Simon B.
Meining, Charles R.
Preffer, John J.
Preffer, Stephen G.

1875
Everhard, John W.
Beeson, Amaziah
Ish, John C.
Osborn, William

1876
Clark, William
Clark, Cornelius C.
Kerr, John

1877
Bestle, Christian
Cornell, Leonidas
Davis, John
Ellsworth, Naomi
Geer, Charles
Hall, Ira
Krueger, Adolph H.
Krueger, William
McIntyre, Josiah W.
Palmer, Joel
Ransom, Henry
Strever, Lloyd G.
Turner, Peter
Wilson, George
Wilson, Seth
Zweck, George

1878
Blinn, Warren
Bradley, James
Caywood, Samuel
Curtis, James
Flora, William S.
French, Selden M.
Huppe, Herman
McCormick, John H.
Newell, William T.

Osborn, Daniel O.
Osborn, Stephen S.
Piatt, James
Shepard, D.L.
Shull, John C.
Stryker, Cornelius
Wray, Chalmon

1879
Bennett, Harry V.
Cole, S. Wayland
Coombs, James M.
Crowell, Sam
Eidson, S.
Farwell, Cyrus
Huppe, Henry
Huppe, Hugo
Shaffer, John W.
Skinner, Laban
Smith, William T.W.
Stewart, Issac N.
Stewart, William R.

1.0   Traces of the American Indians

Since the end of the last ice age 11,300 years ago, Northern Colorado has been inhabited by humans. First, the Clovis hunters arrived followed by the Folsom culture, then more recent tribes migrated into the area including the Ute, Lakota, Apache, Comanche, Kiowa, Arapaho and Cheyenne.

In the years prior to the arrival of the Euro-Americans, tribes of Arapaho and Cheyenne made their home on the plains that sprawled east from Colorado's northern Front Range. Rivers, such as the Cache la Poudre and the Big Thompson, as well as creeks like the Little Thompson, all fed into the South Platte River. These channels provided water and cover for the game animals the tribes hunted. The creek bottoms were also the sites of large encampments of teepees such as the one trapper Antoine Janis reported near present-day Laporte in 1844.

While the Arapaho and Cheyenne lived on the plains and came to rely on horses for transportation, the Utes resided in the mountains to the west and, for the most part, traveled on foot. The tribes seldom trespassed upon their rivals' territory, although the Utes were known to venture to the plains and steal horses from the Arapaho and Cheyenne.

By the late 1860s, as homesteaders began to claim farms and ranches in the Little Thompson Valley, the Cheyenne, Arapaho and Ute were seldom seen, each tribe withdrawing to the north where there were fewer white men.

Though the early homesteaders of the Little Thompson Valley may not have seen many American Indians, they encountered evidence of the natives' seasonal occupation of the area. The settlers' descendants made hobbies of collecting artifacts—arrowheads, awls, scrapers, and grinding stones—left behind at campsites along the banks of the Little Thompson River. Traces of ancient burials were found in the foothills that formed a narrow margin between the rolling valley and towering peaks less than 10 miles distant.

Albert Beeler, a boy when his family came to the Red Rock District west of Berthoud in 1880, was one of the first local residents to amass a large collection of Indian artifacts from the Little Thompson Valley. His wife, Emma Flora Beeler, was the daughter of early pioneer William S. Flora. Together they built an extensive collection that included a large number of arrowheads.

The sons of Swedish immigrant James Jensen—Roy, Bill, Jim, and George—also made a pastime of arrowhead hunting in the foothills of the Little Thompson Valley. The collections of Jim and George Jensen, now in the possession of the Berthoud Historical Society, contain many artifacts collected in the Little Thompson Valley beginning in the late 1920s. (The Jensens also collected in the Casper, Wyoming area where their brother, Roy, became interested in the hobby while working as foreman at the Campbell sheep ranch.)

One of the Jensens' favorite locales to hunt for artifacts was the valley where Blore Lake, a marshy wetland, was located in the foothills west of Berthoud. Nestled in the gulch behind present-day Carter Lake Dam No. 2, the bank surrounding the marsh was where one of the brothers would creep along in an automobile while his siblings perched on the running boards and picked up flint points.

Another productive collecting area was in the vicinity of the present-day marina at the north end of Carter Lake. Numerous fire rings scattered across a south-facing slope indicated large Indian encampments. The site of the camp was inundated when Carter Lake was completed by the Bureau of Reclamation in the early 1950s.

One of Jim Jensen's most unusual archaeological finds was the remnants of a Plains-Woodland Indian pot he discovered near the old stagecoach road that ran between Loveland and Estes Park. Now in the collection of the University of Colorado Museum of Natural History in Boulder, the rare conical-shaped clay vessel was made during that tribe's presence in the area between 300 and 900 AD.

In the spring of 1916, while plowing on Harry Bennett's farm on the Little Thompson river bottom a mile south of Berthoud, William Frazier discovered a shallow grave filled with human remains. Frazier's discovery included skeletons and skulls that had been randomly cast into the grave. Since the bones were not accompanied by items such as buttons or coins, they were suspected to be those of early American Indians. When Frazier told Bennett about his discovery, Bennett recalled an old Indian trail that came down into the Little Thompson Valley from the upper Buckhorn. In the past Bennett had "found many stone arrowheads, beads and other implements and trinkets lost by the red men on their journeyings."

The *Berthoud Bulletin* reported in July 1932 that a group of local boys, including brothers Sam and Carl Hertha and Charles Graves, discovered an Indian grave in a gulch four or five miles west of town. The burial site contained fragments of bones, flint arrowheads and grinding stones.

Eventually the various native Northern Colorado tribes departed the area. We continue to unearth remnants of the life they left behind.

Ansel Watrous, *History of Larimer County, Colorado*, The Courier Printing & Publishing Company, Fort Collins, Colorado, 1911, p. 15.

Frances Nielson, Helen Fickel, *The Heritage of Berthoud and the Little Thompson Valley*, Helen McCarty Fickel, Berthoud, Colorado, 1992.

Berthoud Bulletin, Mar. 17, 1916; July 28, 1932.

1.1   Chief Friday and the Arapaho

Before the arrival of the white man, the Little Thompson Valley was just a small sliver of an Arapaho tribal homeland that sprawled from northern New Mexico to South Dakota. On that land the nomadic tribe hunted buffalo on horseback and made winter camps along rivers and creeks. The Arapaho were among the first native inhabitants to come in contact with the Euro-Americans who flooded into the region after the 1858 gold discovery near present-day Denver.

Historic accounts indicate that a small Arapaho band led by Chief Friday made camps in the Cache la Poudre, Big Thompson and Little Thompson river drainages. Another band led by Chief Ni Wot or "Left Hand" called the area around Boulder and St. Vrain creeks their seasonal home. The Arapaho considered Estes Park to be their hunting grounds and defended it from the Utes who occupied the mountains to the west.

Chief Friday

Friday's association with the white man began in 1831 when fur trader Thomas Fitzpatrick discovered three lost Indian boys wandering along the Cimarron cutoff of the Santa Fe Trail. The boys were starving after being separated from their band. Fitzpatrick took a liking to one of the boys who was about five years of age. He named him Friday because he found him on that day. Later Fitzpatrick sent Friday to St. Louis to be educated but eventually reunited him with his tribe when an Arapaho woman recognized him as her lost son. The fate of the boys Fitzpatrick discovered with Friday is unknown.

After Friday rejoined the Arapaho, he became well known to

white men who were impressed with his ability to speak English. In 1844, Friday was among the Arapaho who met wanderer and writer Rufus Sage when he stayed at Lupton's Fort on his way to St. Louis. After an outbreak of Indian violence resulted in the death of Ned Brush in 1868, Chief Friday was among the Arapaho who vanished from Northern Colorado and reappeared at Wyoming's Wind River Reservation.

Chief Ni-Wot

The Arapaho Project: *www.colorado.edu.csilw/arapahoproject/contemporary/ history.htm*

Ken Jessen, "Soldiers Rescue Ute Susan from Arapahoe Indians," *Loveland Reporter-Herald*, Dec. 2, 2002.

Diane Brotemarkle, *Old Fort St. Vrain*, pp. 22-41.

1.2   Horse Stealing Raid on the Little Thompson

The American Indians' seasonal habitation of the Little Thompson Valley was drawing to a close by the time the first homesteaders arrived in the late 1860s. For that reason, there are few accounts that chronicle early encounters between settlers and Indians.

One incident came to light on March 26, 1937, when an article in the *Lyons Recorder* described a horse-stealing raid that occurred near present-day Lyons. It is likely the event transpired around the time of the last Indian hostilities in Larimer County in the 1860s. The article was authored by N.C. Sullivan,

David Lykins

who had interviewed David Lykins, a witness to the raid years earlier.

Lykins, a miner-turned-rancher, had settled in the foothills of the Little Thompson Valley when a band of Indians drove off horses belonging to settlers living along the creek. The settlers, including Lykins, grabbed their guns and followed the raiding party on foot to Brackett Gulch where Lykins managed to shoot the party's chief at dusk.

The settlers hiked home in the darkness and went to Longmont the following day to secure horses and follow the Indians' trail. Unable to make up ground, the men traveled many miles into the "Black Hills" north of Laporte before they abandoned pursuit. A few years later Lykins claimed to have found the location where he killed the chief. There he retrieved a bullet-pierced skull, tomahawk, bow and arrows, and an elaborate horse bridle decorated with Spanish silver.

It is possible that the raid involved Utes who as noted earlier occasionally made horse raids on Arapaho and Cheyenne camps in the same area. Raiding parties from that tribe came into conflict with settlers living along the Cache la Poudre in 1862 and the Big Thompson rivers in 1864.

Lyons Recorder, Mar. 26, 1937.

Ansel Watrous, *History of Larimer County*, Colorado, The Courier Printing & Publishing Company, Fort Collins, Colorado, 1911, p. 47.

1.3   Trappers and Traders

The Big and Little Thompson rivers were named during the fur-trapping era. While the namesake of the rivers remains a mystery, it is certain the rivers were known by those names in 1843. That year, Lieutenant John C. Fremont conducted his second expedition to the region and cited the rivers in a report to the United States War Department.

Larimer County historian Ansel Watrous speculated that the Thompson rivers were named for English engineer and astronomer David Thompson. Thompson traversed the area under the auspices of the Northwest Fur Company in 1810.

Watrous noted, "Trappers camps were established by the Northwest Fur company, later known as the Hudson Bay Company, on all the streams of Northern Colorado, during the second decade of the nineteenth century, and it is quite possible that the camps on these two streams were known and designated as the Big and Little Thompson camps."

Another possible namesake of the rivers is trader Phillip Thompson. E. Willard Smith mentioned Thompson in an account of his travels to Fort Vasquez and Brown's Hole in 1839. Fort Vasquez was located in the vicinity of present-day Platteville, Colorado.

In the 1820s, when beaver hats were the height of fashion, a bustling fur trade drew trappers to Northern Colorado where rivers were teeming with beaver. These trappers set their trap lines on streams, including the Little Thompson, and bartered pelts in exchange for goods at trading posts along the South Platte River.

The South Platte River takes water from the Little Thompson after it merges with its sister river, the Big Thompson, near present-day Milliken. The forts or trading posts along the South Platte included Fort Lupton (est. 1836), Fort Jackson (est. 1837), Fort Vasquez (est. 1835) and Fort St. Vrain (est. 1838). The forts were located on the "Trappers Trail" that stretched from Taos, New Mexico to Fort Laramie, Wyoming.

Ansel Watrous, *History of Larimer County*, Colorado, The Courier Printing & Publishing Company, Fort Collins, Colorado, 1911, p. 17, 171.

Lee Whiteley, *The Cherokee Trail: Bent's Old Fort to Fort Bridger*, Johnson Printing, Boulder, Colorado, 1999, p. 7.

Percy Stanley Fritz, *Colorado The Centennial State*, Prentice-Hall Inc., New York, New York, 1941, p. 95.

1.4   Fremont Camps at the Confluence of the Thompson Rivers

In May 1843, less than a year after completing his first survey of the Rocky Mountains, Lieutenant John C. Fremont of the U.S. Corps of Topographical Engineers embarked on a second expedition that led him through present-day Larimer County. Fremont's destination was the unexplored region south of the Columbia River.

Fremont's second expedition departed from Kansas Landing (near present-day Kansas City) on May 29, 1843. His 40-man party included William Gilpin of Missouri, who later became the first Territorial Governor of Colorado. Armed with carbines and a 12-pound howitzer, Fremont's men traveled with 12 mule-drawn carts filled with provisions and equipment.

After reaching Fort St. Vrain on the South Platte River, Fremont extended his exploration south to Pueblo then re-traced his path to Fort St. Vrain and continued on, making camp at the confluence of the Big and Little Thompson rivers north of present-day Milliken on July 26, 1843.

Before departing Fort St. Vrain, Fremont had inquired about mountain passes that would allow his party to cross the Rocky Mountains from present-day Larimer County. In his report to the War Department, Fremont lamented that he was unable to find anyone who knew about such a mountain pass because the few trappers who once lived in the area had moved on.

Lieutenant John C. Fremont

Cutting across the hogbacks north of the mouth of the Cache la Poudre, Fremont's expedition came into the valley of the North Fork of the Cache la Poudre and continued northward along the Rockies to South Pass in Wyoming where they crossed the Continental Divide. Later that year Fremont's party reached the Pacific coast.

Ansel Watrous, *History of Larimer County, Colorado*, The Courier Printing & Publishing Company, Fort Collins, Colorado, 1911, p. 23.

Stephen C. Schell, *Following John C. Fremont's Trail Through Northern Colorado 1843*, Citizens Printing, Fort Collins, Colorado, 2010, pp. 74-81.

1.5   The Cherokee Trail Traverses the Little Thompson Valley in 1850

In 1849, a party of gold seekers from Arkansas cut away from the Santa Fe Trail and traveled north along Colorado's Front Range to join the Oregon-California Trail in southern Wyoming. This party, known as the Evans Company, included more than a dozen Americanized members of the Cherokee Nation who intended to prospect in California's gold fields. Their route became known as the Cherokee Trail.

Evans's train of about 40 wagons traveled past Bent's Fort on its way up the Arkansas River to Pueblo. From Pueblo they continued north on the old Trappers Trail, passed the remnants of Fort St. Vrain, and crossed the South Platte River near its confluence with the Cache la Poudre River east of present-day Greeley. Traveling along the north bank of the Cache la Poudre River, they veered north along the base of the foothills and proceeded toward the Laramie Plains where they joined the Oregon-California Trail.

In 1850, another party of Cherokee gold seekers known as the Edmonson Company followed Evans's trail. Unlike Evans, the Edmonson Company forded the South Platte River in the vicinity of present-day Denver. Heading north, they blazed a wagon road along the base of the foothills, crossing Coal Creek, Boulder Creek and the St. Vrain, Little Thompson and Big Thompson rivers. After they crossed the Cache la Poudre River, they re-joined the trail Evans used in 1849.

The Edmonson Company's guide was mountain man Ben Simon, who was part French and part Delaware Indian. He was accompanied by his wife who was part Spanish and part Snake Indian, and her brother and mother, full-blooded Snake Indians. A young girl related to Simon's wife drove a small herd of milk cows.

James Mitchell, a member of the Edmonson Company, kept a diary. On Friday, June 14, 1850, Mitchell noted the party crossed "another bad creek" (St. Vrain River), and hunted antelope on their way north. He added that Simon's brother-in-law was injured during the pursuit of a wounded antelope.

Near evening, Edmonson's company forded "another daingerous <sic> bad creek" (Little Thompson River) and made camp for the night. In his diary, Mitchell wrote that Simon referred to the river as "sadly creek" because he had found a saddle on its banks long ago.

In the following days, the Edmonson Company crossed the Big Thompson and Cache la Poudre rivers. In present-day Wyoming, Simon guided the company due west over a new wagon route, across the Laramie Plains, to shorten the distance of their trip to the California gold fields.

On Friday, June 21, 1850, a group of three men including diarist and sketch artist William Quesenbury, traversed the Little Thompson Valley in an attempt to catch up with the Edmonson Company. A short time later, the McNair/Taylor Company of 14 wagons and ox teams led by "captains" Oliver and Holmes followed the road the Edmonson Company had blazed along the foothills.

Patricia K.A. Fletcher, Dr. Jack Earl Fletcher and Lee Whiteley, *Cherokee Trail Diaries, Vol. II—1850 Another New Route to the California Gold Fields*, Sequim, WA: Fletcher Family Foundation, 1999, p. xxii.

1.6   Cattle Drives up the Cherokee Trail

After the first parties of gold seekers from the Cherokee Nation had established a wagon road along Colorado's Front Range in 1849 and 1850, the route was heavily used for cattle and sheep drives from Texas and Arkansas to California.

In June 1854, a cattle drive conducted by Calvin Holmes and 18 drovers pushed through the Thompson valleys. Holmes's drive originated in Benton County, Arkansas, and pushed past large herds of buffalo in modern-day Oklahoma and Kansas. After crossing the South Platte River at the site of the future town of Denver, Holmes pointed his herd north, following the route pioneered by the Edmonson Company in 1850.

On June 13, 1854, Holmes's cattle drive reached the Big Thompson River. There a bolt of lightning struck and several of Holmes's horse teams, cattle, and men were knocked to the ground. A cowboy by the name of H.L.W. Peterson was killed. Holmes noted in his diary that Peterson was buried in a "mound on the prairie."

A few days later, William Engels's company followed Holmes through the Thompson valleys. Engels reported, "...came to camp on Thomson's Creek [Little Thompson River]...(and) a larger stream (Big Thompson River)...the awfullest <sic> place for musquitoes <sic> that I ever saw."

Arthur Pendry Welchman and a party known as the Texas Mormons crossed the South Platte River near present-day Denver in August 1854 and continued north on the route pioneered by the Edmonson Company in 1850. Several more Mormon parties followed Edmonson's route on their way from Texas to Utah that year.

In a diary entry dated August 12, 1854, Welchman mentioned that his party encountered two graves while traveling

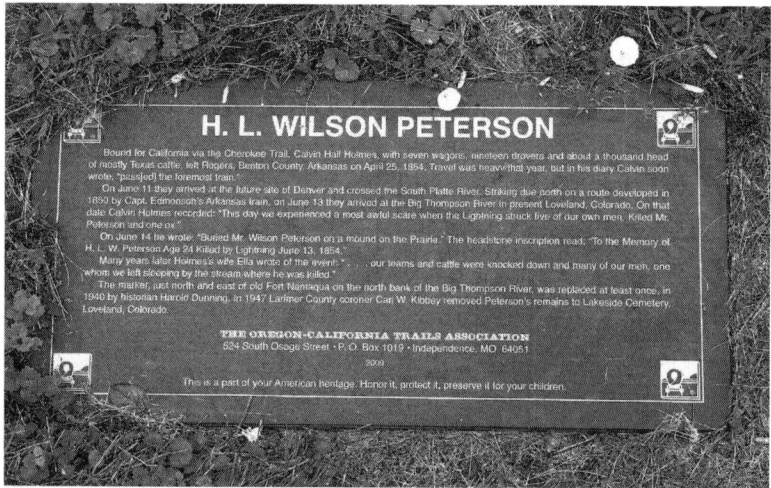

In 2008, the Oregon-California Trails Association placed a plaque on H.L. Wilson Peterson's grave in Loveland's Lakeside Cemetery. (Mark French)

north from Cherry Creek, although he did not identify the locations of the graves. One grave may have been the "mound on the prairie" where H.L.W. Peterson was laid to rest on the north bank of the Big Thompson River. It is possible that the second grave may have been on the bluff north of the Little Thompson River crossing.

Patricia K.A. Fletcher and Dr. Jack E. Fletcher, *Cherokee Trail Diaries, Vol. III — 1851-1900 Emigrants, Goldseekers, Cattle Drivers, and Outlaws*, Sequim, WA: P.K.A. Fletcher and J. E. Fletcher, 2001, pp. 90-91.

1.7   Grave at Little Thompson Crossing

Dr. Jack K. Fletcher and Patricia K.A. Fletcher, authors of *Cherokee Trail Diaries*, speculated that there were three graves Welchman's party may have seen as they traveled north from Cherry Creek.

One grave may have contained J.R. Todd who was buried near Owl Canyon, north of present-day Fort Collins. Todd died following a skirmish with Indians in 1852. Another grave might have been H.L.W. Peterson's final resting place near the Big Thompson River. The third may have been that of Theodore F. Wheeler and an assailant named Brown—both buried in a common grave near present-day Denver in the summer of 1854.

A fourth possible grave, not identified by the Fletchers, is a burial site located on the bluff north of the Little Thompson River three miles southwest of present-day Berthoud, Colorado.

The grave, located above the Little Thompson river bottom, lies in close proximity to the ford where the 1862 stagecoach road used by Ben Holladay's Overland Mail & Express Co. crossed the stream. Previously the road was known as the Cherokee Trail. It is possible the occupant of the unmarked grave may have been a member of one of the emigrant trains or cattle drives that passed through the Little Thompson Valley after the Edmonson party blazed that segment of the Cherokee Trail in the spring of 1850. The occupant of the grave is not identified in any known diary.

In August 2009, the "Little Thompson Crossing Grave" was capped with a large sandstone marker and covered with stone cobble by members of the Howard Malchow family (property owners) and volunteers from the Berthoud Historical Society.

Information regarding the location of the grave and the

Little Thompson Crossing Grave located three miles southwest of Berthoud, Colorado, on the bluff north of the Little Thompson River. (Mark French)

Little Thompson Crossing had been passed down through the years by early pioneers, tenant farmers, and property owners. Depressions in the hillside suggest the possibility of multiple graves at the site overlooking the river crossing and the campground used by early travelers.

It is suspected that the Little Thompson Crossing Grave is one of the first, if not the first, burial of a non-American Indian in the Little Thompson Valley. The first documented interment in the Little Thompson Valley occurred on January 21, 1884, at the site that later became Berthoud's Greenlawn Cemetery.

Patricia K.A. Fletcher and Dr. Jack E. Fletcher, *Cherokee Trail Diaries, Vol. III — 1851-1900 Emigrants, Goldseekers, Cattle Drivers, and Outlaws*, Sequim, WA: P.K.A. Fletcher and J. E. Fletcher, 2001, *p. 108.*

Frances Nielson, Helen Fickel, *The Heritage of Berthoud and the Little Thompson Valley*, Helen McCarty Fickel, Berthoud, Colorado, 1992.

1.8   Heavy Travel on the Cherokee Trail

In 1856, Ellen Hundley kept a diary of her family's journey against the west-bound flow of wagons on the Cherokee Trail. The Hundleys were returning to Texas from Utah.

While traveling south from the Thompson valleys, the Hundleys encountered the fourth California-bound wagon train they had met since leaving Utah. At the crossing of the South Platte River near present-day Denver, they saw two additional wagon trains from Arkansas. Near Cherry Creek they met two more parties driving a thousand head of cattle in the opposite direction as the Texas-bound family was traveling. By the time the Hundleys approached the Arkansas River, they had seen 11 westbound trains in 11 days.

The U.S. Army also made heavy use of the Cherokee Trail. In

March 1858, Captain Randolph B. Marcy transported supplies and drove livestock over the trail on his way from Fort Union, New Mexico, to Fort Bridger, Wyoming. Marcy's orders were to supply troops that had been sent there to quell the Mormons' bid for independence from the federal government.

Marcy joined forces with Colonel Loring at Cherry Creek. In May 1858, their combined force passed through the Thompson valleys on its way north. Marcy's party consisted of 30 wagons and more than a thousand animals. Loring's command included nearly 350 soldiers. Upon arriving at Fort Bridger, Marcy joined forces with Colonel Albert S. Johnston. They marched into Salt Lake anticipating Mormon resistance but encountered none.

In the fall of 1858, George Andrew Jackson, a miner returning from California, stopped at a trapper camp near the foothills along the Big Thompson River. The camp had been set up by Nicholas and Antoine Janis. In 1860, the *Rocky Mountain News* announced that a new town, Miraville City, had been laid out at that location. Mountain man Mariano Medina stayed in one of the cabins, remaining at this location until his death in 1878, thus becoming the first permanent settler in the Big Thompson Valley.

Horace Greeley, editor of the *New York Tribune*, traveled the Cherokee Trail from Denver to Fort Laramie in the spring of 1859. At Boulder Creek, Greeley's party met four wagons loaded with gold seekers who had given up on Colorado. They were moving on to the gold fields of California.

On his way north, Greeley crossed "...two deep, swift, steep-banked creeks" which were the St. Vrain and Little Thompson rivers. His party rested for breakfast on the banks of the Little Thompson before traveling on to "...the other fork of Thompson's Creek" (Big Thompson River). At that location they met an emigrant company that included several ox-drawn wagons and a herd of more than 200 cattle.

304. Bears' Cathedral near the Big Thompson.

Mariano Medina at the Devil's Backbone west of present-day Loveland, Colorado. (John Carbutt stereoview courtesy of Bill Meirath)

During the summer of 1859, news of gold strikes in the Pikes Peak region captured the world's attention. The following year gold seekers flooded into the area. They traveled every road, including the Cherokee Trail, on their way to seek fortunes in the Rocky Mountains.

Patricia K.A. Fletcher and Dr. Jack E. Fletcher, *Cherokee Trail Diaries, Vol. III — 1851-1900 Emigrants, Goldseekers, Cattle Drivers, and Outlaws*, Sequim, WA: P.K.A. Fletcher and J. E. Fletcher, 2001, pp. 29-31, 131, 138-139, 211-220, 253, 257.

Horace Greeley, *An Overland Journey from New York to San Francisco in the Summer of 1859*, University of Nebraska Press, Lincoln and London, 1999, p. 16.

1.9   During the Gold Rush

By 1860, the Cherokee Trail had become a heavily traveled thoroughfare from the Southeast to the Pikes Peak mining district. While many gold seekers set their sights on the diggings near Denver, a large number went to South Park and the Blue River to prospect.

A steady flow of travelers also continued north on the Cherokee Trail to the gold fields of California. In May 1860, California-bound traveler Philander Powell commented, "At all times in the day we can see wagons, teams, people and droves of cattle and mules."

Upon Powell's arrival in Denver on July 5, 1860, he observed that the settlement was comprised of 600 to 800 houses and a similar number of tents and wagons. Powell's party proceeded to Clear Creek where they paid a 50-cent toll to use the bridge spanning the stream.

As Powell continued north from Clear Creek, he noted, "...there are 600 soldiers camped." The following day after traveling through the St. Vrain and Little Thompson valleys Powell added, "We covered 15 or 16 miles today and through the day we met soldiers in abundance."

Powell's party camped for the night at the Big Thompson River. The following day they reached the Cache la Poudre River where they paid a 50-cent per wagon toll to use the bridge that crossed the river. At that location near present-day Laporte, Powell made note of a "little town" (Colona) and observed, "Indians were in abundance there."

Patricia K.A. Fletcher and Dr. Jack E. Fletcher, *Cherokee Trail Diaries, Vol. III – 1851-1900 Emigrants, Goldseekers, Cattle Drivers, and Outlaws*, Sequim, WA: P.K.A. Fletcher and J. E. Fletcher, 2001, pp. 264-269.

1.10   Cherokee Trail Becomes the Overland Trail

In the spring of 1862, Indian raids in Wyoming between Fort Laramie and South Pass nearly caused Ben Holladay's Overland Mail & Express Company to cease operation. That summer Holladay received the Postmaster General's permission to re-route his mail and passenger service to avoid the hostilities. Beginning at that time, Holladay's stagecoaches left the trail at Julesburg and followed the South Platte River to Latham City at the mouth of the Cache la Poudre River. After crossing the South Platte at Latham, the coaches joined the Cherokee Trail and traveled in a northwesterly direction along the Cache la Poudre. They followed the road until it intersected the original mail route at Fort Bridger.

Major John Kerr, a Holladay employee, led an expeditionary party to Bridger Pass to determine the viability of this new route. After Kerr confirmed its suitability, he was promoted to the position of superintendent of the line between Denver and Salt Lake. Years later, Kerr staked a homestead claim in the Little Thompson Valley.

In July 1862, Camp Collins was established near the banks of the Cache la Poudre River near present-day Laporte. Manned by soldiers from the 9th Kansas Cavalry, the camp served as their base of operation while they protected the stage road from Denver to Fort Halleck in present-day Wyoming.

Camp Collins was destroyed by a flood in June 1864. Five months later the post was reconstructed on higher ground four miles downstream and was named Fort Collins for its commanding officer, Lt. Col. William O. Collins. In 1867, the threat of Indian hostilities and mail robberies along the trail subsided to the point that President Andrew Johnson ordered the post to be abandoned.

In September 1862, Ben Holladay instructed his agents to

Lieutenant William O. Collins

"...change the route from its present course [Latham to Laporte], to one bearing via Denver to Laporte." The new route provided Denver with regular mail delivery. The stagecoach road north from Denver to Laporte followed the trail established by the Edmonson Company in 1850. Holladay's stagecoach road, henceforth known as the Overland Trail, brought stagecoaches packed with mail and passengers rumbling through the Little Thompson Valley.

Patricia K.A. Fletcher and Dr. Jack E. Fletcher, *Cherokee Trail Diaries, Vol. III – 1851-1900 Emigrants, Goldseekers, Cattle Drivers, and Outlaws*, Sequim, WA: P.K.A. Fletcher and J. E. Fletcher, 2001, pp. 287-289, 296.

Louise Bruning Erb, Ann Bruning Brown and Gilberta Bruning Hughes, *The Bridger Pass Overland Trail*, Journal Publishing Company, Greeley, Colorado, 1989, p. 11, 27.

Dorothy Large, *Old Burlington*, St. Vrain Publishing Company, Longmont, Colorado, 1984, p. 18.

1.11   Little Thompson Station

After the route of the Overland Mail & Express Company was extended to Denver in the fall of 1862, a series of stage stations was established along the road north to Laporte. The stations were located every 10 to 15 miles so coaches could change to fresh horse teams.

Stations established to provide a stop for changing teams were called "swing stations." Swing stations generally consisted of a small house or a barn with living quarters. There was also a log corral that held up to 25 horses and mules. Stations where passengers ate meals or stayed overnight were known as "home stations." These larger stations were positioned about every 50 miles.

In 1862, the first stop north of Denver, Child's station, was established south of present-day Broomfield. The second stop, Boone's station, was sited on the banks of Boulder Creek 12 miles north of Child's station. Eighteen miles further up the road was Little Thompson station. An additional eight-mile journey brought coaches to Big Thompson station. Reaching Laporte required another 16 miles of travel. Over time more stations were added or existing stations were relocated or renamed.

Pioneers of Little Thompson Valley monument southwest of Berthoud upon its dedication in 1937. (Berthoud Historical Society)

Little Thompson station, a swing station established in the fall of 1862, was located on the banks of the Little Thompson River southwest of present-day Berthoud. In 1937, a group of local residents dedicated a stone monument in that vicinity to honor the "Pioneers of the Little Thompson." At that time an old settler named Charles L. Wilson noted, "The Overland stage road...came down onto the Little Thompson and crossed the creek just a few rods west of this marker, and on the old campground many relics have been found." The monument honoring the pioneers was located at the northwest corner of the intersection of Highway 287 and West County Rd 4. The marker was later moved to Berthoud Town Park.

The division superintendent who oversaw operation of the stations along the section of the line that included Little Thompson was Jack Slade. A notorious character, Slade was based at the Virginia Dale home station near the present-day Colorado-Wyoming line.

In 1886, the *Fort Collins Courier* published a report about Jack Slade's visit to the Little Thompson station in 1862. The newspaper recounted: "The following interesting reminiscences of Slade, who in an early day was the terror of the mountain region have been unearthed by the *Loveland Reporter*. All the old timers of this valley remember Slade—some of them to their sorrow—and one of them at least, Hon. W.C. Stover, of this city, saw him hung.

"A party of old-timers was congregated at White's the other day when someone mentioned the name of Slade, the former terror of the stage line. Frank Bartholf immediately spoke up, 'I received my introduction to Slade,' he said, 'over on Little Thompson at the stage station. Slade was coming down over the line from his station at Virginia Dale, and at Laporte he got drunk. Between Laporte and Big Thompson he began firing down through the top of the coach and the four passengers rolled out on to the prairie. Slade drove into the Big Thompson station and, going inside, ordered the agent, Roswell, to make him up a cocktail. A loaded shotgun stood in the corner. Slade picked it up and cocked both barrels, covered Roswell with it and ordered the drink mixed in such a manner. Hardly able to hold anything, his hand shook so, Roswell did as directed. Slade then ordered him to come from behind the counter and place the drink on the end of the shotgun, which he did, the two barrels of the gun staring him in the face all the way. After drinking Slade mounted the stage and ran the horses over to the Little Thompson station, when one of them laid down, played out. I was keeping the station for my brother-in-law, who had gone up into the hills to bring down his wife. As the stage drove up I went out to unhitch the horses. The driver made some remark to me and I answered him pretty short. Biff! Something struck me across the right eye. I turned quickly and looked straight into the barrels of

Jack Slade (undated sketch)

Virginia Dale "home station" operated by Jack Slade. (Fishback)

Cherokee and Overland Trails with stage stations
Drawn by Kenneth Jessen
(Based on a map developed by the Oregon-California Trails Association)

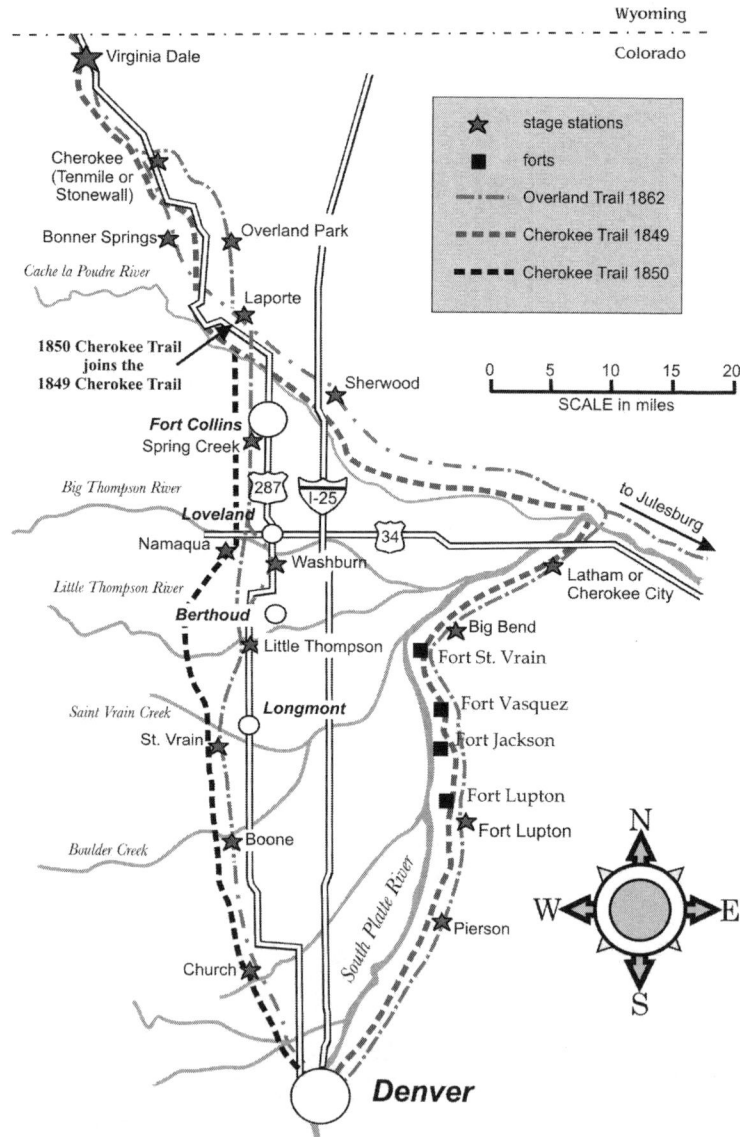

two revolvers. I had never seen Slade before, but I knew right away that we were introduced. After I went into the stable he went over to where a couple of young fellows were camped and threatened to shoot one of their horses, and finally did shoot a dog laying under their wagon. Then he kicked their coffee pot over, put out their fire and went off. All this time two fellows with guns stood there and watched him. He afterwards wrote me a letter of apology, saying he thought I was the agent, and he did not allow any of his agents to cuss him."

Slade was dismissed from his position with the Overland Mail & Express Company for drunkenness in November 1862. He relocated to Virginia City, Montana, where he was lynched by vigilantes two years later.

Louise Bruning Erb, Ann Bruning Brown, Gilberta Bruning Hughes, *The Bridger Pass Overland Trail 1862-1868*, Journal Publishing Company, Greeley, Colorado, 1989, pp. 25-27.

J.V. Frederick, *Ben Holladay the Stagecoach King*, University of Nebraska Press, Lincoln and London, 1940, p.291.

Elizabeth Lawrence, *People and Places on the Overland Trail*, Red Mountain Press, 2000, p. 37.

Rocky Mountain News, Nov. 13, 1862.

Fort Collins Courier, Sept. 2, 1886.

1.12 Land Surveys and Homestead Act Bring Settlers

In 1861 and 1863, survey parties under the supervision of John Pierce established the standard parallel and township lines of the Little Thompson Valley. Pierce held the position of "Surveyor General of the Public Lands of the United States in the Territory of Colorado."

In the fall of 1864, a crew led by Deputy Surveyor William Ashley conducted the subdivision survey of the Little Thompson Valley. Ashley, the crew's compass man, supervised a party that included flagman William H. Shafford, chainmen Samuel Y. Case and W.S. Case, and boundsman John W. Case. From October 27 to November 8, 1864, they surveyed Township 4 N. R. 69 W. of the Sixth Principal Meridian in Colorado. Charred cottonwood stakes and rocks were used to mark section corners.

In his survey notes, Ashley rated the Little Thompson Valley as "level and 1st rate." He graded the upland as "good pasture" and identified cottonwood trees as the only timber. He also observed an undergrowth of willows along the meandering river.

Ashley charted two north-south roads on his survey map. In his notes he identified the eastern-most road as the "Stage Road to Denver." It ran through sections 10, 15, 22, 27 and 34 and followed the general route of present-day U.S. Highway 287.

Ashley did not name the western-most road that ran along the base of foothills. The unnamed trail crossed sections 5, 8, 17, 20, 30 and 31 and followed the approximate course of present-day Larimer County Road 23E.

Ashley's subdivision survey and the Homestead Act of 1862 cleared the way for settlement of the Little Thompson Valley. Ashley's 1864 survey designated section lines that made it possible to establish claims with proper boundaries. The Homestead Act allowed citizens and individuals who had filed for citizenship to claim up to one-quarter section of land (160 acres) and required that they set about improving it over five years occupancy to gain ownership.

Ashley's 1864 map and report.

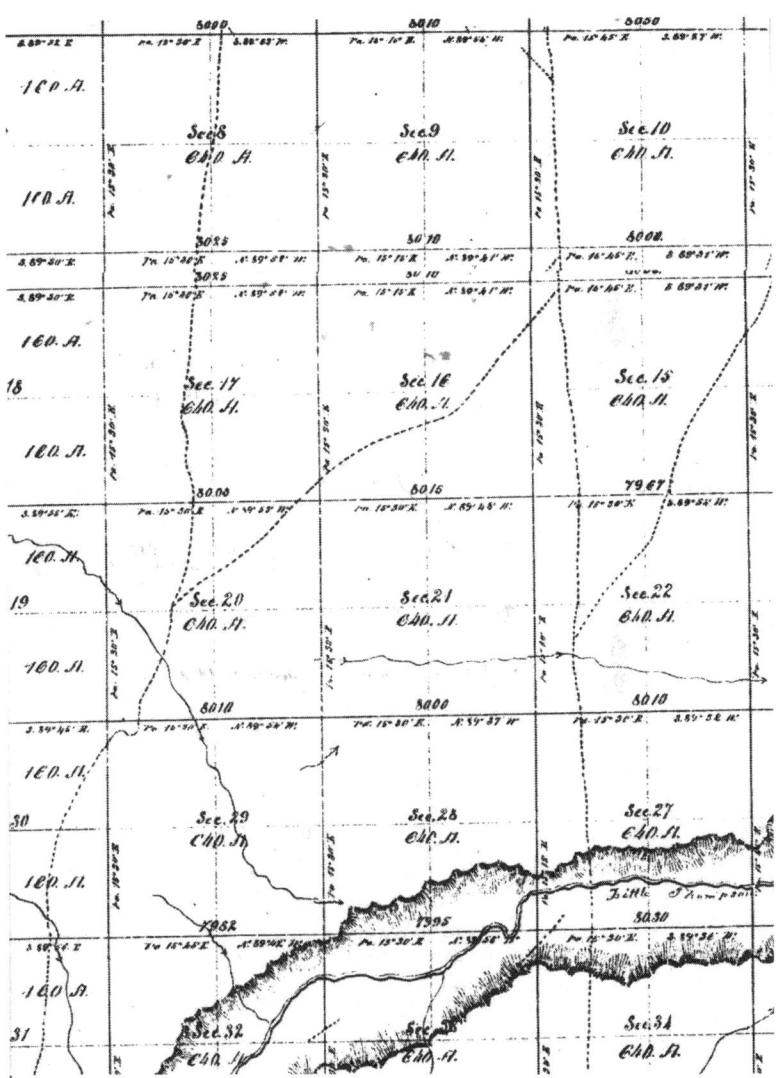

Segment of William Ashley's 1864 survey map of Township 4 N. R. 69W.

1.13   Overland Mail & Express Co. Sold to Wells Fargo

In 1866, stagecoaches stopping at Little Thompson station began carrying the name Wells Fargo & Co. That November, Ben Holladay sold his enterprise after suffering severe financial losses during the Indian wars of 1864 and 1865.

Shortly after the transfer in ownership, a German traveler named Johann Henrich Schmidt stopped at Little Thompson on his way south.

In his diary, Schmidt noted:

"From 1:30 to 3 pm we stopped near the Big Thompson Settlement. It is a small village with a Smithy, a Hotel, Saloons. However I was unable to purchase any bread. There is an Indian corn field here and a small creek nearby. I fried some Elk meat with bacon and coffee and fill my canteen with it. We cross Big Thompson Creek below the Tollbridge 30 to 50 ft wide and 1 ft deep, good water, little snow on the road, 60 degr. There is a 2" covering of snow on both sides, more in the mountains

Seth of Colorado by James Otis Kahler, 1912

which are now as close as 5 miles distance. 5 pm it is getting colder after sundown and is now 47 degrees. Shortly after, we camped at Little Thompsons'. Very little around to make a fire with, had to use my wood reserves. But with good water available I made coffee and fried 4 cuts of bacon mixed crackers and water in and had some pretty good soup. From 7-8 pm I warm myself together with others at the stove in the Ranch House which was located besides a small saloon. No wind outside but freezing. To night I sleep inside wagon I under blankets nice cozy and warm. In the morning between 2 and 3 am it rained some several times.

"Thursday Nov. 15th 1866: Up at 6 am, breakfast and train started at 7 am. 5 wagons of Davis each pulled by 4 mules, in addition about 12 mules walking loose beside the train. 2 other wagons also went along with our train. 42 degr. crossing Little Thompson Creek 10-12 ft wide, but only 3-4" deep. To the left is Little Thompson Station; the road is good and the weather some better. Along the way we saw some wolves to the left and right, however they remained too far away to be shot at..."

Under the operation of Wells Fargo, Concord stagecoaches passed through the Little Thompson Valley three times each week on the 596-mile journey from Denver to Salt Lake City. Along the route were 51 stage stops, 12 of which were "home stations" where overnight accommodations were provided. After departing Denver, teams were changed at "swing stations" located at Churches, Boulder, Burlington (St. Vrain), Little Thompson, Big Thompson (Namaqua), and Spring Canyon before stopping at Laporte for the night.

In August 1867, Wells Fargo added a stage line from Laporte to Cheyenne. As a result, corrals at stations between Denver and Laporte were upgraded to accommodate 40 horses so that two or three coaches would be able to cover the route each day.

On October 1, 1869, Wells Fargo announced plans to sell its stage lines and move exclusively into the express business. Wells Fargo had adapted its operations to the new transcontinental railroad built by the Union Pacific, but the timing was right to move on to other enterprises.

.J.V. Frederick, *Ben Holladay the Stagecoach King*, University of Nebraska Press, Lincoln and London, 1940, pp. 260-261.

Diary of Johann Heinrich Schmidt journal, 1866, Utah Historical Society.

W. Turrentine Jackson, *Wells Fargo in Colorado Territory*, Colorado Historical Society, Denver, Colorado, 1982, pp. 17, 24, 39.

1.14   The Trail in 1867 and 1868

In the fall of 1867, Wells Fargo & Co. hired Joseph Rist to supply hay to the stage stations at Little Thompson, Namaqua (Big Thompson), Spring Canyon, and Laporte. Rist provided wild hay that he harvested from meadows on the Big Thompson and Cache la Poudre river bottoms.

Rist owned land on the north bank of the Big Thompson River near Namaqua that he purchased from Mariano Medina for $700. Wells Fargo & Co. leased Rist's land for one dollar per year and built a large livery barn there.

According to Lucas Brandt, an early pioneer who observed the stage line in operation, eight horses were kept in reserve at each station. A four-horse hitch was generally used to pull stagecoaches, but in cases of rough terrain or muddy conditions, a hitch of six horses was used.

In 1867, Brandt and Louis Papa (Mariano Medina's stepson) passed through the Little Thompson Valley while hauling loads of shingles, lumber and hay with a yoke of oxen. In a diary entry dated August 3, 1867, Brandt noted that he discovered that the bridge over the Little Thompson had been washed away. Later Brandt was hired to haul logs from Blue Mountain so the bridge could be rebuilt. It is likely this bridge was on the unnamed and western-most road identified on Ashley's 1864 survey map.

Lucas Brandt

John Robinson's Circus & Menagerie, the first such troupe to visit the Colorado Territory, may have traveled through the Little Thompson Valley in the summer of 1867. Robinson lunched at Rock Creek station near present-day Lafayette and performed at Laporte that year. The circus featured trick horses and several clowns among nearly 100 performers.

An unidentified correspondent for the *Rocky Mountain News* also passed through the Little Thompson Valley in November 1867, making his way on foot along the Wells Fargo road from Cheyenne to Denver. The correspondent wrote, "Leaving Laporte at nine o'clock, we again turned our faces southward, with the intention of making Little Thompson, twenty-eight miles distant, by nightfall. We stopped at Big Thompson a few minutes for dinner, and had a pleasant chat with the landlord, who posted us on the farming capacities of this valley, and again started on our way. Night found us at Little Thompson with feet heavy and worn. We passed a pleasant evening listening to quaint stories from other guests, men of varied experience, of rough exteriors, but warm hearts. At this point we observed a good view of Longs Peak which is forty miles to the westward, and raises his hoary head in the air, and over whose summit the clouds seem stopping to kiss away the snows."

Generals Ulysses S. Grant, Philip Sheridan, and William T. Sherman passed through the Little Thompson Valley in 1868 after stopping at Namaqua on their way south to Denver. Frontiersman Kit Carson also traveled through that year on his way to Washington D.C.

Years later, the valley's pioneers recalled that the Little Thompson River crossing had also served as a campground for teamsters from the Big Thompson and Cache la Poudre valleys who hauled fresh produce to Denver and the mountain mining camps.

Lucas Brandt, "Pioneer Days on the Big Thompson," *Colorado Magazine 7*, (September 1930) p. 181.

Mary Hagan, *Larimer County Place Names*, Old Army Press, Fort Collins, Colorado, 1984, p. 65.

James D. Hutchison, *Survey and Settlement*, Morrell Graphic Communications, Lafayette, Colorado, 1994, p. 46.

Louise Bruning Erb, Ann Bruning Brown and Gilberta Bruning Hughes, *The Bridger Pass Overland Trail*, Journal Publishing Company, Greeley, Colorado, 1989, p. 27.

Rocky Mountain News, Nov. 26, 1867.

Zethyl Gates, *Mariano Medina Colorado Mountain Man*, Johnson Publishing Company, Boulder, Colorado, 1981, pp. 61-66.

Fort Collins Courier, May 23, 1879.

1.15   The Trails Give Way to Roads

Emigrants continued to use the trails through the Little Thompson Valley into the 1870s and '80s. Several decades later William H. Turner, son of Berthoud town founder Peter

Turner, recalled the heavy wagon traffic on the western-most and unnamed trail on Ashley's 1864 survey map. According to Turner, "The old Texas-to-California trail was going strong at that time [1877], and at many times we would see emigrant trains one-half mile long or longer. It ran about four miles west of the present town of Berthoud, crossed the Little Thompson at Blore's Ranch and the Big Thompson at Namaqua."

Turner also mentioned the "old Burlington-to-St. Louis road" that ran past his family's homestead house at the present site of Berthoud in 1877. (Burlington and St. Louis were early settlements located in close proximity to present-day Longmont and Loveland.) The Turners' homestead house was located at the northwest corner of the present-day intersection of 1st Street and Mountain Avenue in Berthoud.

Turner recalled that the Burlington-to-St. Louis road was also a route used by emigrants. In 1932 he wrote, "I can remember when there would be six to ten covered wagons in a group going through, and nearly always they camped at the northeast

Peter Turner (left) and family members at their homestead house on the bluff north of the Little Thompson river bottom. (Berthoud Historical Society)

corner of 1st and Mountain Ave. Among such wagon trains was the Sim Jefferes family..." The Jefferes family arrived in the Berthoud area in 1886 and remained for many decades.

With surveys completed and farms fenced by homesteaders, the old trails gave way to roads that followed section lines. The responsibility for determining routes of the first roads fell to local residents appointed as "road viewers" or "road overseers" by the Larimer County Commissioners. In 1876, homesteader Lewis Cross became the first resident of the Little Thompson Valley to serve as a county commissioner.

Frances Nielson, Helen Fickel, *The Heritage of Berthoud and the Little Thompson Valley,* Helen McCarty Fickel, Berthoud, Colorado, 1992.

Ansel Watrous, *History of Larimer County, Colorado,* The Courier Printing & Publishing Company, Fort Collins, Colorado, 1911, p. 125.

1.16   The First Settlers

Homesteaders started to stake claims in the Little Thompson Valley in the mid-1860s. The first claims bordered or straddled the river where it emerged from the foothills. Shaded by towering cottonwood trees and thickly carpeted with wild hay, these meadows were the finest homesteading sites in the valley. Tipi rings in that vicinity were evidence that tribes of American Indians had also favored the area at an earlier time.

William R. "Dick" Blore, Cary Culver and John Mahoney were among a handful of men to settle in the Little Thompson Valley in the 1860s. Like many other early arrivals, they came to Colorado during the gold rush to Pikes Peak.

Dick Blore, a native New Yorker, came to Colorado in the fall of 1858. In June 1859, Blore, along with David Horsfal and Matthew L. McCaslin, discovered the famous Horsfal lode at

Gold Hill. The men formed the Gold Hill Mining Company with Blore acting as president.

When the Horsfal mine needed a large stamp mill to crush ore, McCaslin and Blore traveled to Denver where they convinced Robert and Cary Culver and John Mahoney to take their new stamp mill to Gold Hill instead of the Gregory District. Over the next two years, ore from the Horsfal lode produced more than $200,000. During that time, Blore also established a livestock ranch near the Pella settlement on the St. Vrain River. In 1861, he sold it to McCaslin who had taken his share of the mine's profits.

After selling his St. Vrain ranch, Blore purchased a military bounty land claim where the Little Thompson River emerged from the foothills southwest of present-day Berthoud. In 1866, brothers-in-law Cary Culver and John Mahoney established homesteads on land west of Blore, their one-time business associate. David Lykins and James M. Eaglin settled in the Little Thompson Valley that year as well.

James Eaglin's homestead cabin still stands near the junction of present-day Larimer County Rd. 17 and the Little Thompson River. (Mark French)

Ranching was the main source of income for Blore, Culver, Mahoney, and Lykins. It was Blore who brought the first Hereford cattle to Larimer County. Having established their ranches, Blore (1866), Culver & Mahoney (1867), Lykins (1868) and Eaglin (1869) filed for water rights from the Little Thompson River in order to irrigate meadows where they pastured their herds. Eaglin's ditch watered the first crop of wheat grown in the Little Thompson Valley.

In addition to improvements such as dams and irrigation ditches, a stone school building was constructed on Blore's ranch in 1877. The first board of the Blore School District consisted of Blore, Culver and Lykins.

McGrath. *The Real Pioneers of Colorado.* pp. 54-55.

Silvia Pettem, *Red Rocks to Riches*, Stonehenge Books, Boulder, Colorado, 1980, pp. 11, 20.

Ansel Watrous, *History of Larimer County, Colorado*, The Courier Printing & Publishing Company, Fort Collins, Colorado, 1911, pp. 132, 95.

Fort Collins Courier, Apr. 19, 1883.

Frances Nielson, Helen Fickel, *The Heritage of Berthoud and the Little Thompson Valley*, Helen McCarty Fickel, Berthoud, Colorado, 1992.

1.17 Cattlemen

Since the flow of water in the Little Thompson River was far less than that of the Big Thompson to the north and St. Vrain to the south, settlers arriving in the region in the 1860s selected claims along the larger rivers first. As a result, several cattle ranchers maintained command of the Little Thompson Valley's open range into the 1870s.

During this era it was reported that Dick Blore and the partnership of Culver & Mahoney ran as many as 3,000 head of cattle on the Little Thompson. Other ranchers including William Stagg and George Zweck also made use of the open range until the 1870s when the organization of reservoir and ditch companies began to draw farmers to the valley with the promise of irrigated land.

Cattle ranching in the Colorado Territory remained loosely regulated until 1872 when the territorial legislature charged each county with the responsibility of organizing round-ups. Prior to that, disputes over unbranded livestock occasionally erupted in gunfire.

In May and June 1872, Larimer County's commissioners ordered eight cattle round-ups to be culminated at "...Carwyle's ranch on the Little Thompson, Mariano's lake on the Big Thompson, the first dry creek north of the Big Thompson on the Fort Collins road, the lake two miles north of Arthur's dry creek east of Round Butte on the Fort Collins road, the bend in the dry creek three miles below Park Station, Jack Springs on the upper Cheyenne road, eight miles up Boxelder creek from the north, and at Indian Springs on the lower Cheyenne road."

"Carwyle's ranch on the Little Thompson," later relinquished and homesteaded by rancher Lewis Cross, straddled the river one mile south of present-day Berthoud.

After each round-up, cattle were separated or "cut" into groups according to brand. The unbranded stock was then set apart in a "caveyard" or "cavey." After the round-up foreman determined ownership of unbranded cattle, the animals were either claimed or turned loose on the open range.

The last county-organized cattle round-up in the Little Thompson Valley was conducted in 1879.

Fort Collins Courier, Jan. 18, 1879.

Fort Collins Express, Jan. 1, 1894.

1.18   Dick Blore

In 1883, William R. "Dick" Blore informed the *Fort Collins Courier* that he'd "...been on the Little Thompson since 1862." If not the first, Blore was certainly among the first settlers in the Little Thompson Valley.

By the 1870s, Blore had increased his land holdings to more than 1,200 acres so that his ranch straddled the Little Thompson River at the Boulder-Larimer county line. Since Blore had established his ranch before there was a settlement in the Little Thompson Valley, he traveled south to communities in Boulder County to conduct his business.

A native New Yorker who converted his mining profits into a sprawling cattle ranch, Blore earned the reputation of being "...a prominent stockman" and "...breeder of fine-blooded stock." In 1881, the *Fort Collins Courier* identified Blore as the owner of "one of the most valuable herds in the state."

In 1885, while the valley's open range was rapidly surrendering to homestead claims, Blore reported that his herds numbered 93 horses and 80 cattle. Blore's neighbor, David Lykins, claimed to own 194 head of cattle while Culver & Mahoney declared their stock to include 54 horses and 99 cattle.

In the 1890s, when Blore was in his early sixties, his health began to fail. He relocated to Denver where he died on January 16, 1902.

Fort Collins Courier, Apr. 19, 1883; Feb. 3, 1881; Mar. 26, 1885.

1.19 Culver & Mahoney

Cary Culver and John Mahoney ran cattle on the open range of the Little Thompson Valley until the late 1870s. Then, like Dick Blore, they turned to raising fine livestock. In 1884, nearly 20 years after Culver and Mahoney arrived in the valley, the _Fort Collins Courier_ described the "model stock farm" they had developed.

The _Courier_ noted: "At the mouth of the Little Thompson canon is a ranch located by Messrs. Culver and Mahoney in 1867. Few places could be found which possess more natural adaptabilities for the business in which they are engaged. With an abundance of clear water, excellent grazing and meadow lands and admirable protectors from winds on all sides, the place from the first gave ample promise of its future possibilities. Today it is one of the best,

Cary Culver (Berthoud Historical Society)

The timber frame barn at the Culver & Mahoney ranch is three stories tall and over 150 feet in length. More than 100,000 wooden shingles were used to cover its roof. (Mark French)

if not the best, arranged stock farms in Colorado. It is conducted in a thoroughly intelligent and business-like manner and is a model which every farmer in Colorado should take the trouble to examine. Among the first objects of interest are the large and conveniently appointed barns and corrals. The barns affording stable room for one hundred head of stock and so constructed as to make breeding and watering an easy matter. Every kind and grade of stock has separate apartments, avoiding any trouble or danger in handling. Among the different animals seen by the *Courier* reporter, were the magnificent imported Percheron stallion Midnight, exhibited at the Larimer county fair, Nazarene, a three-year-old imported stallion, Wamba, an imported four-year-old Percheron and Duke of Kent, an imported Clydesdale. These are all horses of the purest blood and cleanest pedigree. Besides these some very fine grade stallions are worthy of notice. Tiger, three-fourth Norman, Dick, a half-breed and several other colts weighing from 1,300 to 1,700 pounds are excellent specimens of their type.

"Brood mares are selected from the very highest grades attainable so that excellent results are shown at the first cross. Messrs. Culver & Mahoney have for some years made a specialty of breeding heavy draft horses and the stock raised shows that they have been eminently successful.

"In the line of cattle raising the experiments of crossing of the Cushman and Devon breeds, has been tried with excellent results, these cattle combining the good-sized frame of the Durham with the round, plump form, dark red color and active qualities of the Devon. About twenty-five head of these steers are being fattened for market this fall. These gentlemen are also engaged in raising hogs by crossing the Suffolk and Poland Chinas. They have some very fine specimens and are well pleased with the experiment. They are fattening their hogs on chopped wheat and alfalfa. Knowing this firm's preference for pure blooded stock one is not surprised at seeing their flocks of uniformly colored Dominick chickens, their forty-three stands of pure Italian bees, nor anything else in fact which adds to the completeness of a model stock farm. The ranch consists of twenty-five hundred acres, all under a substantial smooth wire fence. It is so divided that just so much grain and general

The front half of the Culver & Mahoney farm house mirrored the back half of the house and served as a residence for the families of Cary Culver and John Mahoney. (Berthoud Historical Society)

farm produce can be raised as will be consumed by different departments of the farm. Besides a large area of meadow grass, one hundred and twenty acres of alfalfa are cut three times each year and fed out to horses, cattle, sheep and hogs either clear or mixed and chopped with grain. A threshing machine, corn sheller, hay cutter and feed mill are operated making the farm independent within itself."

The writer concluded, "The farm house itself is a large, handsome, stone structure elegantly furnished with all modern conveniences. There is a clean, substantial business like look about the whole place, and with the excellence of all its departments it may well be called a model stock farm."

Fort Collins Courier, Nov. 27, 1884.

1.20 Settlement in the 1870s

In the early 1870s, large tracts of land in the valley above the Little Thompson river bottom remained unclaimed. The prime land straddling the river had already been reserved and improved by pioneers such as Lykins, Blore, Culver, Mahoney, and Eaglin.

A number of settlers who arrived with those men in the 1860s canceled or relinquished their homestead claims before they proved up. Among them was Elza Phillips who came in 1866 and cancelled in 1869. William and Oliver Carwile staked claims along the Little Thompson River in September 1869 but relinquished in August 1873. For two years prior to relinquishing the Carwiles had operated a toll bridge over the river.

Other settlers who arrived in the early 1870s were Joseph Musgrove (1870), James Smith (1870), William K. Staggs

(1870), George Cronk (1872), Lewis Cross (1872) and Matthew Carter (1873). Many of these early arrivals traveled along the South Platte River from Julesburg to Denver at a time when conflict with American Indian tribes posed a serious threat to their lives.

Most of the early settlers used the Homestead Act of 1862 to obtain farms and ranches. They began by paying a $10 filing fee to establish a claim on up to one-quarter section (160 acres) of land. They were then required to construct a dwelling that measured no less than 12 by 14 feet and to cultivate the land over a five-year residency to earn a patent (deed of title). Some of the homesteaders "commuted to cash" and paid $1.25 per acre to obtain their patent before five years had passed. Having done so, they were subsequently able to sell their homesteads to interested buyers.

Others purchased public land that had been granted to the Union Pacific Railroad (successor to the Denver Pacific Railway). The land was sold by the railroad company in order to raise funds for the expansion or construction of its lines. What

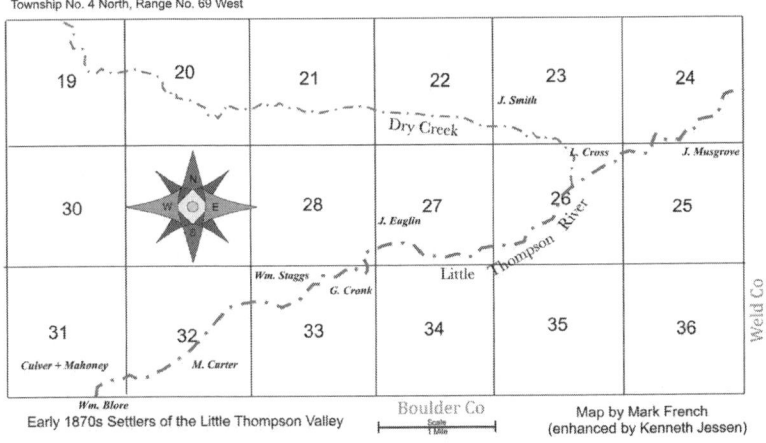

Land lying along the Little Thompson river bottom was the first to be claimed in the early 1870s. (Mark French and Kenneth Jessen map; larger version at end of book)

the homesteaders termed as "railroad land" was sold to them at rates and terms they considered favorable. Various railroad acts passed by Congress kept the cost of land to little more than a dollar per acre.

A few settlers obtained land by purchasing military bounty land warrants issued as incentives for enlistment during the War of 1812. Most of the warrants were not actually used by the war veterans (or their heirs) but instead sold to others who used them on unclaimed public land.

Early homesteader James Eaglin purchased a General Land Office Warrant in 1871 from the widow of Nicholas Teal who had fought with Pick's Company, Virginia Militia, during the War of 1812. With Teal's warrant, Eaglin obtained the patent to a 160-acre ranch straddling the Little Thompson River two miles below the claim he established in 1866.

As early as 1872, farms in the valley commanded a handsome price. In October of that year an advertisement in the *Longmont Press* announced: "A farm of 160 acres on the Little Thompson bottom, with house, field fenced and in crop. All under ditch and first-rate land. Price $2,000."

Longmont Press, Oct. 2, 1872.

Frances Nielson, Helen Fickel, *The Heritage of Berthoud and the Little Thompson Valley*, Helen McCarty Fickel, Berthoud, Colorado, 1992.

PART 2

BERTHOUD
ON THE RIVER BOTTOM

Berthoud and Surrounding Area

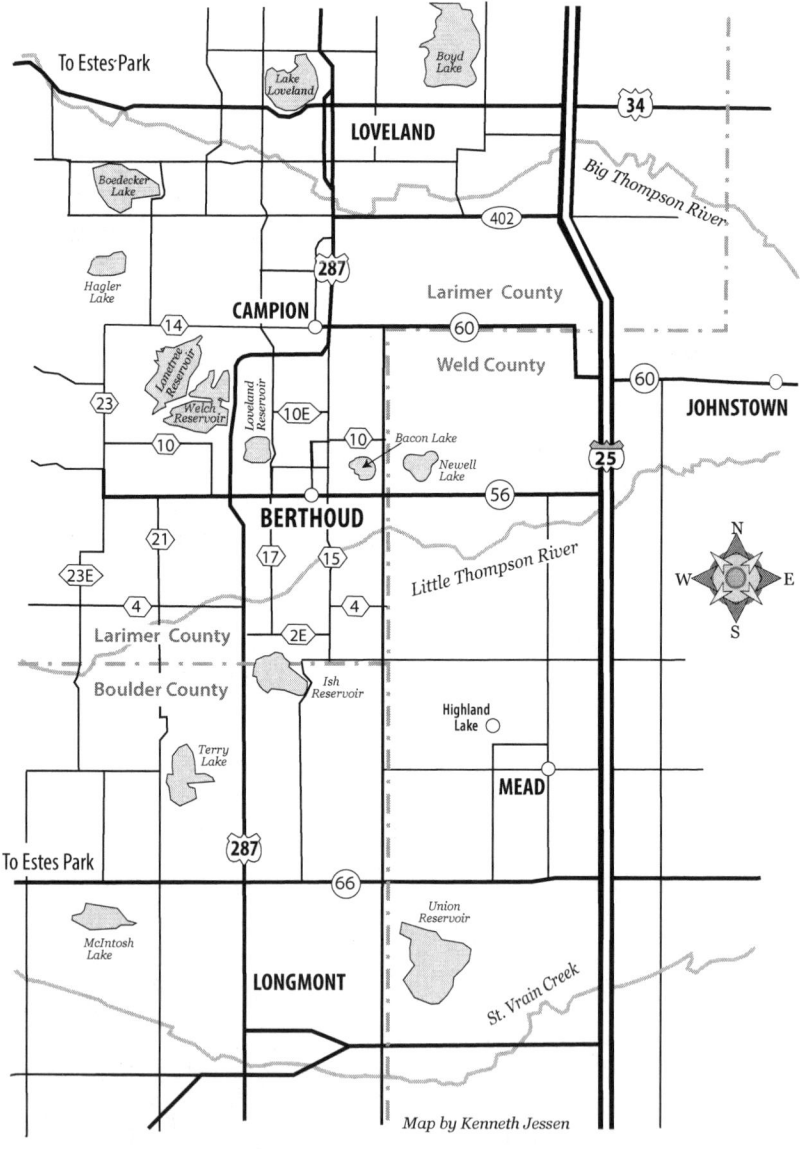

Map by Kenneth Jessen

2.0   The Arrival of Lewis Cross

A handful of homesteaders began to stake claims along the banks of the Little Thompson River in the late 1860s, but it wasn't until Lewis Cross arrived in 1872 that a community started to develop. It came to be called Little Thompson. In 1872, Cross, who had been ranching on Ralston Creek near the Territorial Capitol of Golden, moved his cattle to a small vale in the foothills of the Little Thompson Valley which later came to be known as Carter's Glade. Cross watered his cattle at a big spring there that was inundated when Carter Lake was constructed in 1954.

In September 1873, Cross moved from the foothills to the fertile Little Thompson river bottom where he staked a homestead claim on an 80-acre ranch straddling the river one mile south of present-day Berthoud. The rolling bottomland Cross selected for his homestead was originally part of two tracts first claimed by William J. and Oliver W. Carwile in 1869.

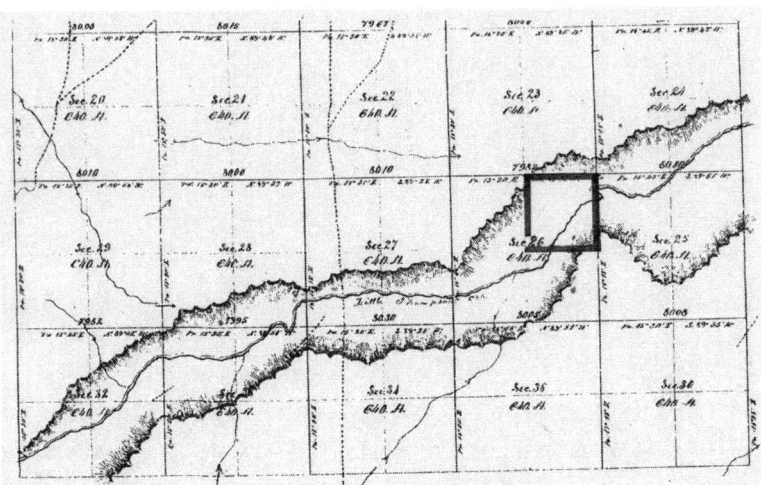

Lewis Cross Homestead in Section 26, Township 4, Range 69W. (Map filed with Surveyor General's Office, Denver, Dec. 23, 1863)

The Carwiles operated a toll bridge over the Little Thompson River until April 1871 when the wooden bridge spanning the creek was purchased by Larimer County for $75. In the spring of 1874, the bridge was repaired and opened to the public. In 1875 the wagon route that traversed the bridge was commonly known as the Longmont to St. Louis Stage Road.

The Carwiles cancelled their homestead claims in August 1873. One month later, Cross filed his own claim on an 80-acre parcel that included the north halves of the Carwiles' properties. Cross proved up on the claim in February 1879. In 1880, Cross homesteaded an additional 80 acres bordering his farm to the south thus increasing his land holdings to 160 acres.

The Homestead Act of 1862 required homesteaders to live on and improve their claims for a period of five years before they gained ownership. It is not known if Cross constructed a new cabin for his homestead dwelling or if he lived in an existing structure built by one of the Carwiles.

Ansel Watrous, *History of Larimer County, Colorado*, The Courier Printing & Publishing Company, Fort Collins, Colorado, 1911.

Homestead records.

Larimer County road records.

1880 Larimer County census.

2.1   Lewis Cross

Lewis Cross was 56 years of age when he came to the Little Thompson Valley in 1872. Born in Virginia in 1816, Cross moved with his family to Indiana where he later married Susanna Maudlin. Their family grew to include children Alvah, John, Sarah and Benjamin while they lived in Indiana and Calvin,

Dillon and William after they moved to Iowa.

At the height of the Pikes Peak Gold Rush in 1860, Cross and his son, Alvah, traveled to Colorado with the understanding that the remainder of the family would follow later. On May 1, 1864, Susanna Cross and the six children who had stayed with her in Iowa joined a four-party wagon train to reunite with Cross and Alvah. Despite crossing the plains at a time when Indian hostility was at its height, they arrived safely in the Colorado Territory seven weeks later on June 18, 1864. One of the young men in the party, 22-year-old George Wilson, married Sarah Cross later that year. Like his father-in-law Lewis Cross, Wilson eventually settled in the Little Thompson Valley.

Lewis Cross and his wife Susanna Maudlin Cross (Berthoud Historical Society)

Wilson later recalled that when their wagon train reached Julesburg, they asked how far it was to the next campground and were told it was another eight miles. While they watered their stock and filled water barrels, a man informed them that their horses were the best to come through that spring. After continuing on the trail a few miles, they found good grass and made camp, tying their horses to their wagons. When they arrived at the campground the next morning they discovered that during the night their stock had been stolen. The men presumed that Indians were to blame. Wilson, however, was sure the man who

George Wilson
(Berthoud Historical Society)

admired their horses at Julesburg was responsible for the theft.

While he established a new life for his family in Colorado, Cross dabbled in mining at Central City. Upon his family's arrival, he took them to that bustling mining camp where they remained for about a year before he purchased a ranch on Ralston Creek near the territorial capitol of Golden. Cross and his family lived there until 1872, then moved about 40 miles north along Colorado's Front Range to the sparsely settled Little Thompson Valley.

By the time Lewis Cross arrived there, the family group had shrunk to his wife Susanna and sons Ben (age 25), Dillon (age 19) and William (age 13). Alvah Cross had died at Central City in 1867. Four older children—Alvah, John, Sarah and Calvin—had established their families elsewhere in Colorado by the time their parents homesteaded.

Frances Nielson, Helen Fickel, *The Heritage of Berthoud and the Little Thompson Valley*, Helen McCarty Fickel, Berthoud, Colorado, 1992.

Iva Wilson, "History of Lewis Cross," unpublished manuscript.

Iva Wilson, "History of George Wilson," unpublished manuscript.

2.2   The Lewis Cross Homestead

When Lewis Cross moved his ranch to the foothills of the Little Thompson Valley in 1872, large tracts of land lay unclaimed.

The St. Vrain Valley to the south and the Big Thompson and Cache la Poudre valleys to the north had already started to populate with farmers who valued these large rivers. In contrast, the Little Thompson Valley remained open range and the domain of cattlemen, even though most of the area's ranchers believed homesteaders were crowding their range. In March 1874 the *Fort Collins Standard* reported, "They already complain that the range is too small, but thousands of cattle are yet ranging on the Buckhorn and Little Thompson creeks and farther up in the mountains in the parks where the Big Thompson, abounding in trout, flows swiftly through the hills."

For his homestead Cross selected a site where the heavily-traveled wagon road between Longmont and Saint Louis [present-day Loveland] crossed Little Thompson Creek. In 1877, the general course of the road became part of the route of the Colorado Central Railroad, which connected the Territorial Capitol of Golden with Cheyenne and was the main line of the Union Pacific Railroad.

Cross built his family cabin on the north bank of the river near the Longmont-St. Louis Road which formed the eastern boundary of his property. There Cross not only had water for his family and livestock but also for travelers who found the Cross homestead a convenient stopping place. Cross and his wife gained a reputation for their hospitality and the old homesteader, with his flowing white beard, came to be known as Father Cross and his wife as Mother Cross.

On June 3, 1874, one year after Cross established his homestead on the river bottom, a reporter from the *Fort Collins Standard* observed, "We took a spin across the divide to Little Thompson and found that much neglected portion of our country flourishing with a large crop in and up. The principal farmers are Messrs. Blower [Blore], Eaglin, Cross and Smith. The grain is looking fine and ditches are in good order. We whiled away a few hours and rested our pony at the hospitable horse camp of 'California George' and ascertained that there has been ready sales all spring for horse stock, mules being in good demand and commanding good prices. We can recommend any desiring tough road stock or the best bottomed 'knotty' saddle ponies in the Territory to give George a call and they can be accommodated. A good substantial bridge has been erected over the creek at Carwile's crossing—a decided improvement on the old lap-sided affair, which was a dread to all freighters on the road; and by the bye, there is a constant and steady increase of travel over this road. The freighters and emigrant trains lining the road make it look like old times."

The principal farmers identified by the *Standard* were William Richard "Dick" Blore, James Eaglin, Lewis Cross and James M. Smith. Blore's homestead was located on the Little Thompson River near the base of the foothills. Eaglin's farm straddled the creek one mile west of the Cross homestead.

Fort Collins Standard, Mar. 18, 1874.

2.3   Organizing School Districts

After Cross staked his homestead claim in 1873, he joined neighboring ranchers Henry Krueger and George Cronk to organize Larimer County School District No. 13, the thirteenth such district to be formed in the county. Its boundaries were established on October 15, 1874, and its status secured with a $5 fee submitted to Larimer County School Superintendent Clark Boughton. In its early years the school was known as the Little Thompson School.

In a report that Krueger filed for the year ending September 30, 1874, he noted that 17 students attended Little Thompson

School. The identity of the first teacher is unknown but Cross, Krueger and Cronk served on the district's first school board as president, secretary and treasurer, respectively.

Classes at Little Thompson were held in a one-room log cabin built by Lewis Cross. The structure measured 12 by 16 feet and sat on the south bank of the Little Thompson River opposite the Cross homestead cabin. The youngest Cross son, William, was 13 years old in 1874 and probably attended the school.

The cabin was also used as a place of worship by early residents who conducted a Sabbath School there. Services were held by itinerant "saddle bag" preachers on missions from the United Brethren and Methodist churches. Community spelling bees and lyceums also took place in the cabin for the entertainment of the families living in the Little Thompson Valley.

After the Colorado Central Railroad was constructed in 1877, officials named the Little Thompson settlement Berthoud

Prior to 1914 when the school was enlarged, the student body of District No. 22 posed with their teacher in front of the brick building constructed in 1882. (Berthoud Historical Society)

The Blore schoolhouse (no longer standing) fell into disuse after 1910 when the district was re-named and the Culver School building was erected nearby. (Berthoud Historical Society)

in honor of the railroad's chief engineer, Capt. Edward Louis Berthoud. After that the school became known as the Berthoud School. In the early 1880s a vigorous debate arose around the best site on which to erect a new school building in District No. 13. Unable to resolve their differences, residents living near the existing school building voted to split from District No. 13 and form District No. 22. In June 1882, District No. 22 constructed a new brick building to replace the log cabin that had served as a school since 1874. The following year a pared-down District No. 13 built the Mars Hill School one mile north of present-day Berthoud.

In 1877, the Blore School District was organized by families living in the area where the Little Thompson River emerged from the foothills. The Blore School sat on a bluff north of the creek about five miles west of the Little Thompson School. The building, constructed from stone quarried on the nearby Cary Culver ranch, was built by mason and homesteader Luther

Hixson. Hixson also constructed an elegant two-story, stone "double-house" for the families of Culver and his brother-in-law John Mahoney. The Blore School District spanned the Boulder and Larimer county line and later came to be known as "Culver Dist. No. 37—Joint." Mary Kilgore was the teacher at the Blore School when it opened in 1877. Dick Blore, Cary Culver and David Lykins served on its first school board.

Lone Tree School District No. 20 was organized in 1880. Located about five miles northwest of Berthoud, Lone Tree School derived its name from a solitary hackberry tree that stood as a landmark on the divide between the Big and Little Thompson valleys. The hackberry was not native to Northern Colorado so the tree's origin was unknown. Since the tree (no longer standing) was located in the vicinity of the Cherokee Trail that came into use in 1850s, it may have been planted by an emigrant traveler.

The Culver School, constructed in 1910, replaced the original Blore School of Joint District No. 37. (Berthoud Historical Society)

The Sunnyside School (no longer standing) was located at the northwest corner of the present-day intersection of Weld County Road 46 and Weld County Road 7. (Berthoud Historical Society)

Sunnyside School District No. 36 was also organized in 1880. Located in Weld County, four miles northeast of Berthoud, the school was attended by the children of farmers who irrigated their crops with water from the Handy and Home Supply ditches. The first school building, a small one-room frame structure, was replaced by a large, two-room, brick building in 1904.

In 1882, Red Rock School District No. 23 was organized in a sprawling area that extended north from the Little Thompson River bottom to Red Rock Glade at the base of the foothills. The first Red Rock School building, a one-room frame structure, was still being built when classes began in the fall of 1882. For that reason, students met in the front room of the nearby Anson Snively home until the schoolhouse was completed. The first teacher at Red Rock, Miss Mate Smith, recalled that she arrived at Berthoud during a fierce windstorm and spent the night with the Lewis Cross family before traveling to Red Rock the following morning.

The Red Rock School building (no longer standing) was constructed in 1882. (Berthoud Historical Society, c. 1912)

The Mars Hill School was built in 1883 after residents living on the Little Thompson river bottom split from School District No. 13 and formed School District No. 22. The school building was originally located at the southwest corner of the present-day intersection of old Highway 287 and Larimer County Road 10E. The country lane that later became Mountain Avenue in Berthoud served as the dividing line between School District No. 13 and School District No. 22. Annie Fairman and Ed Willis were early teachers at the Mars Hill School, which in 1887 was moved north to Campion to be used by Summit School District No. 54.

Located two miles northeast of the original Berthoud settlement in Weld County, Whipple School District No. 18 was also organized in 1883. While the school building was being

The building that housed the Mars Hill School and subsequently the Summit School in present-day Campion is located at 2349 South Garfield, Loveland. It fell into disuse when the Summit School was built in 1919-20. (Mark French)

constructed at the northeast corner of Judge Marvin Delos Whipple's homestead farm, classes met in his granary. Miss Effie Moore was Whipple's first teacher. Many Whipple teachers boarded with families living in the district.

A pair of gentle bluffs that rise from the horizon six miles northeast of Berthoud gave their name to Twin Mounds School District No. 38 sometime around 1885. Originally part of the neighboring Sunnyside School District, the Twin Mounds School District hired Loveland contractor J.M. Cunningham to build a new frame school house, which he completed in January 1886. Located in Weld County and on the divide between the Big and Little Thompson valleys, the Twin Mounds School was also used in the 1880s and 1890s for United Brethren Church services.

The original Whipple School was located at the southwest corner of the intersection of present-day Highway 56 and Weld County Road 3. (Berthoud Historical Society)

Frances Nielson, Helen Fickel, *The Heritage of Berthoud and the Little Thompson Valley*, Helen McCarty Fickel, Berthoud, Colorado, 1992.

Loveland Reporter, Aug. 21, 1884.

2.4 Ministry in the Little Thompson Valley

In 1873, Davis Johnson Baxter established the community's first Sunday school in the little log school house on the Little Thompson river bottom. Baxter, a Union veteran of the Civil War, had a homestead one mile east of the school in Weld County.

Prior to Baxter's arrival in the valley, the United Brethren church had already established its presence in Northern Colorado. In the fall of 1869, the United Brethren Board of Missions began sending its ministers to the area at the request of Big Thompson homesteader David Hershman. In 1872, Rev. William Hamilton McCormick was appointed to the "Big Thompson Mission" and charged to minister to settlers in "...a field of operation from Denver to the Cache la Poudre." United Brethren "saddle bag preachers" such as McCormick traveled on horseback and conducted church services in homes and schools.

In his capacity as an itinerant United Brethren minister, Reverend William H. McCormick was well-known to the early settlers of Northern Colorado. (*Berthoud Bulletin*)

Years later, McCormick recalled, "From 1870 to 1884, I knew almost every family in the Clear Creek, Boulder, St. Vrain, Little and Big Thompson and Cache la Poudre valleys...I lived for years literally in the saddle, carried my blanket and lariat, so that when night came the earth was good enough for my weary limbs to rest upon, and I fell asleep gazing upon the starry firmament."

In 1874, the United Brethren Board of Missions officially added Little Thompson to the Big Thompson Mission and appointed Rev. H. Archaret as its pastor. Rev. W.P. Caldwell succeeded Archaret.

Reverend Elkanah J. Lamb relocated to Estes Park after a lean year in the Little Thompson Valley. (*Past Memories and Future Thoughts*)

In 1877, the United Brethren assigned Rev. Elkanah Lamb to Little Thompson but a plague of grasshoppers reduced farmers' incomes to the point where there was little money to support a minister. Lamb relocated to Estes Park where he established a dairy and earned additional income by guiding climbers to the summit of Longs Peak. Reverends M. Harry, William H. McCormick and J.W. Zimmerman succeeded Lamb in the Little Thompson Valley.

Upon his arrival in the Little Thompson Valley in 1878, Stephen D. S. Osborn helped Baxter conduct a Sabbath School. His father, William H. Osborn, with the help of itinerant Methodist ministers who were also passing through the area, held church services at Little Thompson as well. United Brethren ministers, however, conducted services on a regular, twice-monthly basis.

Baxter, a pious man whose faith was tested on all accounts, came to the valley with his wife Susan and young daughter in 1873. A son, Samuel was added to the family in 1875. The boy's mother died in February 1876. Their daughter, six-year-old Agnes Eustace, followed her in death in 1877. Samuel died at the age of 10 in January 1886. All were laid to rest in the

Burlington Cemetery near present-day Longmont, Colorado. Baxter remarried and played a leading role in the development of the community. Baxter died in 1908 and was buried east of Berthoud at the Greenlawn cemetery he had helped establish in 1884.

As Lewis Cross had done, Osborn subsequently left the homestead he had established on Ralston Creek near Golden to sink roots in the Little Thompson Valley. In the 1860s when Osborn and his family traveled across the plains from Iowa, his father, William H. Osborn, insisted that the wagon train remain camped on Sundays so he could preach throughout the day. Stephen and Margaret Osborn were members of the United Brethren congregation which built the first church building in the new town of Berthoud in 1886.

Davis J. Baxter relied on his strong faith to withstand the loss of his wife and children at his Berthoud homestead. (Berthoud Historical Society)

Stephen S. Osborne was the son of United Brethren minister William H. Osborn. His father was among the party of pioneers Osborne led to the Colorado Territory in 1860. (*Berthoud Bulletin*)

McCormick, Rev. W.H., "A Life Story of the Late Rev. W.H. McCormick."

Berthoud Bulletin, Feb. 11, 1932.

Berthoud Bulletin, "Pioneer Edition," Sept. 7, 1901.

Frances Nielson, Helen Fickel, *The Heritage of Berthoud and the Little Thompson Valley*, Helen McCarty Fickel, Berthoud, Colorado, 1992.

Rev. Elkanah J. Lamb, *Past Memories and Future Thoughts*, United Brethren Publishing House, 1905.

2.5   Stagecoach and Mail Service to Little Thompson

In February 1875, the *Rocky Mountain News* announced that a stagecoach service that would run three days each week between Longmont and Fort Collins was ready to operate. The Cross homestead was on the main road connecting the two communities. This marked the first regular stagecoach service carrying passengers and mail through Little Thompson where the Cross cabin sat on the north bank of the river.

This stagecoach route was documented in 1877 when neighbors of Cross, including John W. Everhard and John C. Ish, petitioned the Larimer County Board of Commissioners to close an existing road that cut through the middle of their farms. The commissioners' notes on the proceedings contain a map identifying the "Longmont-St. Louis Stage Road" (present-day Larimer County Road 15B) as running along the eastern boundary of the Cross homestead.

From 1875 to 1877, when the stagecoach line was in operation, a large barn on the Cross homestead was used as a stage barn. The building may have been constructed for that purpose. In the *History of Lewis Cross*, written by his descendant, Iva Martindale Wilson, it was noted, "The mail was carried through from Denver to Cheyenne by a four-horse stage. During storms or when the roads were bad, six or eight horses were driven."

In February 1875, Cross made successful application to the United States Post Office Department to establish the Little Thompson Post Office, the sixth to be founded in Larimer County. On April 5, 1875, Cross was named Postmaster of Little Thompson by the administration of President Ulysses S. Grant. He was paid an annual salary of $12. Cross collected mail from the stagecoaches and kept it in a cigar box stashed in his cabin. Local homesteaders periodically came from their farms and ranches to pick up their mail.

In 1877, when the Colorado Central Railroad completed its Longmont-Cheyenne extension past the Cross homestead, mail delivery shifted from stagecoach to train. That's when the name of Little Thompson was changed to Berthoud. On April 4, 1878, Cross was appointed Berthoud Postmaster by the administration of President Rutherford B. Hayes. In the winter of 1878-79, Cross built a new two-story brick dwelling on his homestead and shifted the post office to the front room of his new home.

A barn at Lewis Cross homestead on the Little Thompson river bottom dates to 1875 when it was used by a stagecoach line running between Denver and Cheyenne, Wyoming. Photo c. 1930. (Berthoud Historical Society)

Rocky Mountain News, Feb. 16, 1875.

Larimer County Road Book R, pp.52-53.

William H. Bauer, James L. Ozment, John H. Willard, *Colorado Post Offices*, Colorado Railroad Museum, Golden, Colorado, 1990, p. 19.

Frances Nielson, Helen Fickel, *The Heritage of Berthoud and the Little Thompson Valley*, Helen McCarty Fickel, Berthoud, Colorado, 1992.

2.6   Boulder and Larimer County Irrigating and Manufacturing Co.

The development of the Little Thompson Valley gained steam in 1875 when the Boulder and Larimer County Irrigating and Manufacturing Company was organized to divert water from the Little Thompson River for irrigation.

When the first homesteaders arrived in the valley in the late 1860s, they staked claims on the creek to secure a water supply for themselves, their crops, and their cattle. Among these early settlers were ranchers Dick Blore, Cary Culver, John Mahoney, David Lykins and George Zweck. The first farmer to raise a crop of wheat in the valley was said to have been James Eaglin in the late 1860s.

In 1867, Culver & Mahoney filed for water rights from the Little Thompson River. They were followed by Lykins (1868), Blore and Eaglin (1869), Charles Meining (1874), the Boulder and Larimer County Irrigating and Manufacturing Company, Steven Osborn and Samuel Caywood (1875).

Eaglin, whose homestead straddled Little Thompson creek, built a dam about a mile upstream and dug a ditch to carry water to his fields. The flow of the Little Thompson was highest when the spring snow melt filled the river so Eaglin's irrigating was limited to that season.

In 1875 Eaglin sold his 320-acre river bottom farm to John Ish. Ish immediately sold the west half of the tract to his brother-in-law, John W. Everhard. Later that year Ish and Everhard were among a group of stockholders who organized the Boulder and Larimer County Irrigating and Manufacturing Company and purchased a lake located on the high ground south of the Little Thompson river bottom. The waters of the lake spread across the Boulder-Larimer county line, east of present-day Highway 287.

The view west across Ish Reservoir presents a grand panorama of Mt. Meeker, Longs Peak and Twin Sisters. Originally built by the Boulder and Larimer County Irrigating and Manufacturing Company, the reservoir is commonly known as Ish Lake. (Mark French)

In 1879, the *Fort Collins Courier* observed, "This lake covers almost a half section of land and will hold seventeen feet of water. It is filled in the early spring by a ditch from the Little Thompson. In the spring time of the year, while snow is melting on the foothills, water is plenty in this stream and the lake may always be filled. This lake is below the Highland and Supply ditches in Boulder County, both of which are at a convenient distance and, from either of which, the lake may be filled. About two miles west of this is another natural lake which has been tapped and the water is now used by part of the neighborhood. All the above described water supply is on the south side of the stream."

The reservoir built by the irrigating company came to be known as Ish Lake. Its construction was a great advancement for farmers living on the southern slope of the valley since it enabled them to capture the spring run-off and store it for use throughout the summer.

In 1878, the Handy Ditch Company was organized to obtain

water from the Big Thompson River for use on the northern slope of the Little Thompson Valley, but on a far greater scale than the Boulder and Larimer County Irrigating and Manufacturing Company.

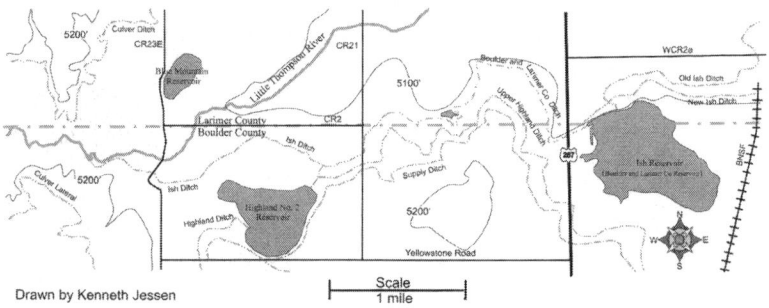

The ditch and reservoir of the Boulder and Larimer County Irrigating and Manufacturing Company is located on the southern slopes of the Little Thompson Valley south of present-day Berthoud. (Map by Kenneth Jessen; larger version at end of book)

Frances Nielson, Helen Fickel, *The Heritage of Berthoud and the Little Thompson Valley*, Helen McCarty Fickel, Berthoud, Colorado, 1992.

Fort Collins Courier, Jan. 18, 1879.

2.7   Ish, Everhard and Kerr

The arrival of brothers-in-law John C. Ish and John W. Everhard in 1875 and John Kerr in 1879 advanced the development of the Little Thompson Valley.

Capt. John Carroll Ish was born in 1839 in Saline County, Missouri. The son of a wealthy farmer and slave owner, Ish enlisted in the Confederate Army in 1861 and mustered out at the end of the Civil War with the rank of captain. During the war Ish was wounded seven times and was held captive for several months in the Federal prison at Alton, Illinois.

After the war, Ish became a cattleman. In 1866, he drove cattle from southern Texas to Independence, Kansas. According to Ansel Watrous in his *History of Larimer County, Colorado*, "In 1869 he [Ish] came to Larimer County, driving 150 carefully selected heifers across the Plains, and these formed the nucleus of a large herd which he ranged on the Buckhorn. The Indians on the Plains were never worse than when he came west, and wagon trains ahead and behind were attacked, and drivers and occu-pants massacred, but the cap-

Capt. John C. Ish was profiled and pic-tured in *The History of Larimer County* published by Fort Collins newspaper-man Ansel Watrous in 1911.

tain with his little party of five, arrived safely at the foot of the Rockies after 90 days of running the gauntlet of warring Sioux and 90 nights of anxious vigil."

In 1875, Ish moved from a ranch in the Buckhorn Valley and purchased James Eaglin's 320-acre farm on the Little Thompson river bottom. Ish sold the western half to his brother-in-law John W. Everhard and kept the eastern half for himself. He farmed there until 1890 when he went to North Park to pursue ranching and mining interests.

During his 15 years in the Little Thompson Valley, Ish helped organize the Boulder and Larimer County Irrigating and Manufacturing Company. He also served on the board of the District No. 22 school at Berthoud that was attended by his children Ewell, Elizabeth, and Virginia. In 1887, his wife Mary acted as the board secretary. The school was located one-half mile east of the Ish farm.

The sisters of John Ish—Susan and Mary—were the wives of John Everhard and John Kerr respectively.

John W. Everhard, a native of Ohio who came of age in Missouri, served in the Confederate Army during the Civil War. In 1875, Everhard brought his wife and young son to the Little Thompson Valley. From his brother-in-law, John Ish, he purchased a 160-acre tract of river bottom land one mile west of the Lewis Cross homestead. Everhard engaged in farming and raising livestock until 1880 when he expanded his operation to include a large ranch near Owl Mountain in North Park. His wife, the former Mary Ish, died there in 1889.

Everhard spent more than two decades in North Park. After his death, his son John B. Everhard remained on the farm southwest of Berthoud where he managed profitable cattle and sheep feeding operations. The younger Everhard was secretary of the Boulder and Larimer County Irrigating and Manufacturing Company for 39 years. He was also one of the organizers of the Berthoud National Bank in 1906.

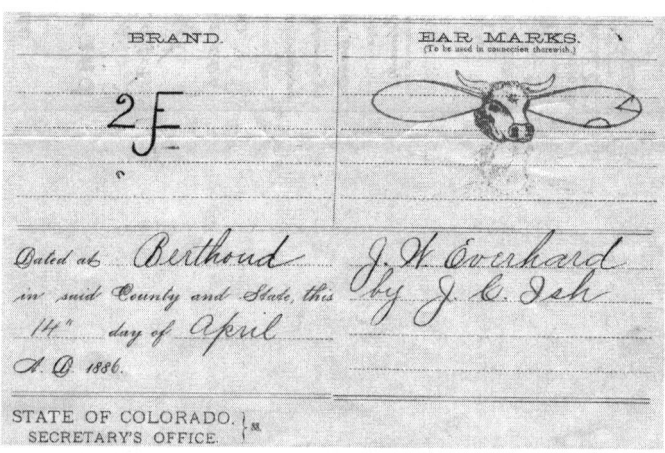

The "Certificate of Stock Brand" John W. Everhard obtained on April 14, 1886, illustrated his cattle brand as "2-J-E." Everhard's son, John B. Everhard, was a partner with his father in the cattle business. For that reason the brand identified two (2) John Everhards (JE). (Mark French Collection)

John W. Everhard's house (no longer standing) was on the south bank of the Little Thompson River at the present-day address of 1528 South Larimer County Road 19. Photo c. 1935. (Mark French Collection)

When John Kerr married Susan Ish in 1864, the region was overrun with prospectors seeking fortunes in the Pikes Peak mining district. Upon Kerr's death in June 1893, the *Fort Collins Courier* recalled, "John Kerr first saw the light May 15, 1823, near Winchester, Virginia, where passed his boyhood days. On coming to man's estate he rejoiced in the possession of a splendid physique, rugged health, a cool brain, a well cultivated and well balanced mind. He was six feet one and a half inches in height, straight as an arrow and well proportioned. His usual weight was 180 pounds."

The *Fort Collins Courier* continued, "His was a brave, adventurous spirit and in early manhood we see him wending his way to the then far west. He arrived in St. Joseph, Missouri, in 1849, just at the height of the overland rush to the California gold fields. The following year he made his first trip across the plains with a train of bull teams loaded with merchandise, billed to Livingston & Kincaid, the pioneer traders of Salt Lake

City. The venture, though extremely hazardous, was successful, and continuing in the business he made a round trip from
the Missouri River to Salt Lake each succeeding year for eight
years for the same firm, his freight bills often running as high
as from $50,000 to $56,000. In 1859 he was engaged in trans-
porting government supplies from Independence, Missouri, to
Salt Lake City for Gen. Sidney Johnson's army, then employed
in keeping the Mormons in subjection. His route lay up the
North Platte via Fort Laramie and the South Pass. It was a wild
country in those days, infested with savages who made frequent
attempts to capture his train, but never with success. His reminiscences of those exciting times were intensely interesting and
if printed would read like a romance.

"While making the crossing at Green River in 1853, he fell
in with Old Jim Baker, W.T. Shortridge and Harvey Jones, the
acquaintance ripening into a warm and enduring friendship.
Of these four intrepid pioneers and frontiersmen but two are
left to recount the thrilling scenes in which they had a part, Old
Jim Baker, who is passing a quiet old age at his home on Snake
river, and Mr. Shortridge of this city.

"Mr. Kerr followed freighting across the plains until the
breaking out of the Civil War and then, disposing of his train,
he came to Denver and engaged in farming and cattle raising.
It was his intention on leaving Salt Lake for Denver to enter
the confederate service, but meeting an accident on the way, in
which one of his legs was seriously fractured, he changed his
mind on recovery and settled down on a farm near Denver. In
1864 he raised the largest crop of wheat ever produced by one
man in Colorado, being 31,000 bushels.

"When Ben Holladay moved the Overland stage line to
Denver in 1863, Mr. Kerr was selected to take charge of the line
from Denver to Salt Lake. He established all the stations on the
road, purchased the stock and supplies and employed the men.
His orders were to see that the mail never failed to go through

on time and he carried them out to the letter. While in charge of the line he never missed a trip or failed in getting the mail through according to contract. Everything was run on a high pressure system in those days. Competent men commanded wages ranging from $200 to $300 per month and everything else was in proportion.

Upon the passing of Major John Kerr in June 1893, the *Fort Collins Courier* published his likeness in addition to an extensive obituary.

"In 1864, Major Kerr married a daughter of Mr. John B. Ish of Saline County, Missouri, who survives him. The ceremony took place in Denver where Miss Ish was then living with her brother...Major Kerr became a resident of Larimer county in 1879, when he located on his beautiful farm, situated on the banks of the Little Thompson creek, about two miles south of Berthoud. Here, until death called him hence, he has enjoyed his declining years the comforts, peace and delights of farm life and the companionship of those near and dear to him, and near here he lies buried. May he rest in peace."

Even though Kerr was 56 years of age when he came to the Little Thompson Valley and had already had a highly successful and varied career, he became active in community affairs. He served on the board of School District No. 22 and was elected president of the Little Thompson Farmers Alliance, formed in 1884 to help local farmers received fair prices for their wheat.

Ansel Watrous, *History of Larimer County, Colorado*, The Courier Printing & Publishing Company, Fort Collins, Colorado, 1911.

Frances Nielson, Helen Fickel, *The Heritage of Berthoud and the Little Thompson Valley*, Helen McCarty Fickel, Berthoud, Colorado, 1992.

Fort Collins Courier, June 29, 1893; Jan. 10, 1884.

2.8   Longmont-Cheyenne Extension of the Colorado Central Railroad

In 1877, the construction of what regional newspapers identified as the "Longmont-Cheyenne Extension" of the Colorado Central Railroad opened northern Colorado and the Little Thompson Valley to development.

That year, the *Boulder County News* reported that the Colorado Central had been chartered in 1865 "...to build a railroad from Golden westward to Black Hawk, Central City, and by the South Fork to Idaho and Empire, thence over the Berthoud Pass to the west boundary of Colorado in the direction of Provo City, Utah." The charter continued, "...and easterly, by Denver, to the east boundary of Colorado, and northeasterly by the coal fields of Jefferson and Boulder counties and the valleys of St. Vrain, Big Thompson and Cache la Poudre, and thence northeast to the northeast corner of Colorado, where the northern branch of the Pacific Railway intercepts said boundary."

In March 1877 William Austin Hamilton Loveland, President of the Colorado Central, instructed his chief engineer, Capt. Edward Louis Berthoud, to immediately begin the preliminary survey for a rail line between Longmont, Colorado, (the northern terminus of the Colorado Central) and Cheyenne, Wyoming. On March 7, 1877, Berthoud started his survey at Longmont progressing, at the rate of about four miles per day. He surveyed a route that the Golden-based *Colorado Transcript* described as "...from Longmont direct to Little Thompson, thence due north to St. Louis, on Big Thompson, then almost in an air-line to Fort Collins." From that point on, the *Transcript* described the route through the northern part of Larimer County as ending at the Union Pacific tracks in Wyoming.

After completing his preliminary survey, Berthoud declared that the route would be not be more than 74 miles in length and that the cost of grading, ties, rail and right-of-way would not exceed $13,000 per mile.

The survey party led by Berthoud established the rail route across the Little Thompson Valley and along the east property line of the Lewis Cross homestead around the middle of March 1877. In a family history, the descendants of Lewis Cross reported that he was a personal friend of Capt. Berthoud. Years earlier Cross had operated a ranch on Ralston Creek near Golden where Berthoud made his home.

Capt. Edward L. Berthoud surveyed the route of the Colorado Central Railroad's "Longmont-Cheyenne Extension." While searching for a possible route over the Continental Divide in 1861, He discovered Berthoud Pass. (Berthoud Historical Society)

Near the end of June 1877, Charles C. Welch, a Colorado Central trustee and an investor, began obtaining a right-of-way from landowners along the course of the Longmont-Cheyenne Extension. Welch would eventually play a key role in the development of the Little Thompson Valley. At that time Chief Engineer Berthoud proceeded to Cheyenne and began working his way back to Longmont, staking the final location of the line as he moved southward. With the goal of having all 74 miles of track ready for rolling stock in 90 days, work on the Longmont-Cheyenne Extension began in July 1877. Contractors Banning & Carr, who had been hired to begin grading at Longmont, brought 50 horse teams to the site within a few days. Simultaneously, the Howlett Brothers positioned 250 teams at Cheyenne to start cut and fill work.

Since the wheat harvest was at its height in July, the Colorado Central promised to hold back on its grading. The

Colorado Transcript noted, "The immense fields of wheat on either side of the railroad line give promise of remunerative freight traffic for the road as soon as it is completed, the whole country from Longmont to Fort Collins for miles and miles on either hand being almost an unbroken field of waving grain, thickly studded with the homes of well-to-do farmers. It is certainly the garden of Colorado."

Anticipating the potential prosperity of the valley, the tabloid added, "A side track is to be put in at Little Thompson for the accommodation of the grain and hay interests, and from the looks of the crops it will be one of the busiest stations upon the whole line." The railroad also made plans to construct a depot at Little Thompson.

On August 22, 1877, the *Colorado Transcript* reported, "There are now upon this work fully 230 teams and 350 to 400 men." That month the firm of Howlett Brothers was also directed to complete the heavy cut and fill work at Little Thompson in preparation for building a 112-foot pile bridge across the creek. The grading of deep cuts through the bluffs north and south of the Little Thompson continued through mid-September when the Colorado Central work force grew to 275 teams and 500 men. At Little Thompson, Howlett Brothers put a "picket and fatigue party" on the heavy work.

In addition to the bridge over the Little Thompson, three other major bridges were constructed under the supervision of J. A. Emrick. Box Elder Creek was spanned with a small bridge that measured 56 feet in length, while the Cache la Poudre and Big Thompson Rivers were spanned by bigger bridges that were 244 and 160 feet long respectively.

By mid-September rails had been laid from Cheyenne to a point nine miles north of Fort Collins at the rate of two miles of track per day. Fifty years later, Bill Turner, whose father owned a homestead north of the Little Thompson River, recalled that the Colorado Central steel gang was putting down track in the vicinity of Berthoud's present-day Bunyan Avenue on October 10, 1877. John McCormick, track boss in charge of the steel gang at that time, later worked as the local section boss and eventually established his own homestead on the bluff northeast of Little Thompson.

On October 24, 1877, the Golden newspaper signaled the near-completion of the line when it noted, "The superstructure of the bridge at Little Thompson was put on yesterday, the approaches are completed and Capt. Reed has a clear run before him across the bridge and into the bluffs on this side, where the Howlett boys are finishing up the heavy work."

On November 7, 1877, the Colorado Central sent its first official train over the Longmont-Cheyenne Extension to inaugurate the state's newest railway.

Later, the *Denver Daily Times* reported, "Mr. Loveland stated that he did not expect the cost to exceed $7,500 per mile with track down, bridges, station-houses, water-tanks, and everything ready for rolling stock. It might possibly reach $8,000 but it was far more likely to fall under than over that first-named figure."

With the Boulder and Larimer Irrigating and Manufacturing Company in place to irrigate farms on the southern slopes of the valley and the Colorado Central's Longmont-Cheyenne Extension ready to link the region with the rest of the nation, the Little Thompson Valley was poised for growth. A system of ditches and reservoirs was still needed to bring water to the northern slopes of the valley, but that project was already in the works.

Boulder County News, Nov. 2, 1877.

Colorado Transcript, Apr. 11, Jun. 27, Jul. 18, Aug. 22, and Sep. 12, 1877.

Frances Nielson, Helen Fickel, *The Heritage of Berthoud and the Little Thompson Valley*, Helen McCarty Fickel, Berthoud, Colorado, 1992.

Denver Daily Times, Oct. 22, 1877.

2.9   Little Thompson Becomes Berthoud

In 1875, when Lewis Cross applied for the community's first post office, he identified its potential location as "Little Thompson." After the post office was secured and regular stagecoach delivery of the U.S. Mail commenced later that year, the tiny cluster of buildings was generally referred to as Little Thompson. These buildings included the Cross homestead cabin, outbuildings, and a log school house.

After the Colorado Central Railroad completed its Longmont-Cheyenne Extension through the valley in 1877, there was discussion among local residents about changing the name Little Thompson to Crossville or La Crosse in honor of Mr. Cross, who by that time was a highly respected and well-known figure in Larimer County. Cross declined and agreed that Little Thompson should be named Berthoud in honor of his friend, Colorado Central Chief Engineer Edward Louis Berthoud.

Years later in 1905, the *Fort Collins Weekly Courier* added another twist to the story surrounding the origin of the town's name when it noted, "When the C&S <sic> road was built in 1877, C.C. Welch, then acting as superintendent of construction, located the town sites north of Longmont and gave names to the towns. Berthoud was named in honor of Capt. Berthoud, a civil engineer associated with Mr. Welch, who is now living in Golden, an aged and respected citizen. It would be a revelation for the Captain to visit the town named in his honor, and see what he is missing by continuing to reside in Golden."

Postal records show that Little Thompson was formally renamed Berthoud in 1878.

Fort Collins Weekly Courier, Mar. 1, 1905.

2.10 Shipping Point in Berthoud

When the Colorado Central Railroad laid tracks through the Little Thompson Valley in 1877, there was great optimism that the newly-named town of Berthoud would become a bustling rail head from which local farmers could ship hay and grain to outside markets. To facilitate that commerce, the Colorado Central constructed a siding there so cars could be set out from the main line while they were being loaded.

The siding was located on the west side of the main tracks and extended north from the bridge that crossed the creek, near the Lewis Cross home. Many years later, Bill Turner, son of homesteader Peter Turner, recalled, "There was a stub switch put in that reached from the creek to the bluff north where trains could pass occasionally."

The siding was adjacent to a town site Cross platted in the late 1870s or early '80s. No map of the town site is presently known to exist. Cross descendants say the town site was located north of Cross's house on the north bank of the Little Thompson River.

During the construction of the Longmont-Cheyenne Extension, the Golden newspaper reported that a depot would be built at Little Thompson, but its construction did not take place upon completion of the line. Miss Mate Smith rode the train to Berthoud in 1882 to take a teaching job at the nearby Red Rock country school. She later wrote that upon her arrival the depot "was nothing but a boxcar perched on a few bricks beside the track." In a letter to the *Berthoud Bulletin* in 1927 E.I. Grenfell of the Colorado & Southern Railroad reported that Jabez Weatherbee was the first depot agent assigned to Berthoud.

Some time prior to the Larimer County census of June 1880, the Colorado Central constructed a section house at Berthoud. The 1880 census indicated that the section house was occupied by the section boss, a housekeeper and three section hands, all natives of Ireland. (Section boss John McCormick was in charge of the steel crew that laid tracks through the valley in 1877. He established a homestead less than a mile east of Berthoud a few years after he left the employment of the Colorado Central.)

The Colorado Central station agent at Berthoud in 1880 was 26-year-old Leonard Kelly. In 1880, three years after the completion of the Longmont-Cheyenne Extension, Kelly may have still been based in the boxcar that served as Berthoud's makeshift depot. In June 1881, the *Fort Collins Courier* noted that Kelly had constructed a comfortable house in Berthoud for his new wife.

Even before the Cheyenne-Longmont Extension was fully complete in November 1877, farmers along the northern stretches of the line were shipping commodities north to Cheyenne. Once the south end of the line was opened to Longmont the farmers of the Little Thompson Valley also began shipping. One of the first shipping reports from Berthoud was recorded in February 1879 when the *Fort Collins Courier* noted, "Times are lively for Weatherbee, the R.R. agent this week. He has sent two cars of hay for J.W. Everhard and John Ish. One car of wheat for Mr. Bennett and one car of hay for Mr. Brush, of Big Thompson."

Davis Baxter, a homesteader living one mile east of Berthoud in Weld County, kept journals in which he concisely recorded his daily activities. Some of his journal entries described hauling family members and farm products to the Berthoud station. One of Baxter's entries, dated March 18, 1880, noted, "...took mother and son to the station." Over the next few years, Baxter logged that he hauled loads of wheat, oats and corn to the Berthoud station and made frequent trips there to check for mail that came in on the train. In 1881, Baxter noted that he purchased products such as flour and ribbon at the Snyder & Grill store in Berthoud and sold the proprietors eggs and butter for cash. Baxter also purchased lumber and coal at Berthoud.

In March 1882 the *Fort Collins Courier* noted that more than 100 carloads of wheat had already been shipped from the Berthoud station that year. A report submitted to Council of Farmers and Millers by Major John Kerr of Berthoud in January 1884 estimated that 100,000 and 150,000 bushels of wheat had been harvested by Little Thompson Valley farmers in 1882 and 1883, respectively.

"Parks threshing outfit," c. 1898. (Berthoud Historical Society)

The *Fort Collins Courier* also noted in December 1883 that the President of the Colorado Central, William Hamilton Austin Loveland, shipped 20 carloads of cattle to Berthoud. Loveland owned a large ranch on a quarter-section of land two miles west of the fledgling settlement.

Loveland and Charles Clark Welch took extraordinary measures to make sure the Colorado Central, in which they were heavily invested, became a commercial success. Both men were keenly aware that the viability of the line would be based on the commerce of prosperous farmers who grew bountiful crops and used the railroad to ship their harvests to outside markets where they could fetch fair market price. For that reason, both

Loveland and Welch not only purchased farms in the fertile Little Thompson Valley, but also worked diligently to organize ditch companies to provide valuable irrigation water for crops.

William Austin Loveland
(*Denver & Vicinity*)

Loveland was born in Chatham, Massachusetts in 1826. Son of a Methodist minister, he worked in a cotton factory and attended college before he entered the army. While working as a teamster during the Mexican War, Loveland was severely wounded at the Battle of Chapultepec. Following the war, Loveland crossed the plains to California where he unsuccessfully prospected for gold. He also prospected in Central America before returning to America where he entered the mercantile business. In 1859, Loveland capitalized on the Pikes Peak gold rush by traveling to Colorado with wagon loads of goods that he used to stock his general store in Golden. As his prosperity increased, Loveland built the first wagon road up Clear Creek Canyon to Black Hawk and helped establish Golden City as the Territorial Capital.

Loveland's desire to promote the development of the Territory inevitably drew him to the railroad industry. In 1865, he was a major investor in the newly chartered Colorado Central Railroad. In 1877, an extension of the Colorado Central line from Longmont to Cheyenne connected the railroad to the Union Pacific Railroad. In the early 1880s, Loveland purchased a farm west of present-day Berthoud that had been a quarter-section of land the United States government awarded to the Union Pacific to stimulate the construction of its railroad.

Loveland's son Frank, who was a prominent lawyer in Denver, oversaw the operation of the ranch and expanded the family's holdings in the Berthoud area.

Loveland profited from cattle and crops raised on his Berthoud ranch, but he gained more from railroad shipping fees charged to farmers sending their commodities to market. Loveland Reservoir, a short distance northwest of present-day Berthoud, takes its name from Loveland, owner of the land where the lake was built.

W.A.H. Loveland's colleague, Charles Clark Welch, was born near Watertown, New York, in 1830. Originally employed as a teacher, Welch found success mining in California and Australia before he migrated to Colorado in 1860. He built and operated profitable quartz-crushing and saw mills in Gilpin, Boulder and Clear Creek counties before he joined the Colorado Central and became one of its trustees. In July 1877, Welch was put in charge of the construction of the Longmont-Cheyenne Extension of the Colorado Central Railroad, a 74-mile rail line that he pushed to completion by November of that year.

Charles C. Welch (*Denver & Vicinity*)

In May 1884, the *Fort Collins Courier* observed, "One of the most extensive farmers of Larimer County is C.C. Welch. Although Mr. Welch's home is in Golden, he is in Larimer county much of the time and may often be found superintending his farms lying south of Loveland. For several years he has been adding more land to his possessions until now he possesses more acres of tillable land than any other one individual in this part of the state. In section 25, lying two miles south of Loveland he owns 280 acres, on which 100 acres of wheat has been put in this spring by a renter. Cornering on this piece is section 35, all of which is owned by Mr. Welch. Nearly the whole section is sown to wheat. Of section 9, lying southwest of 35, Mr. Welch owns 480 acres, 170 of which are sown to grain. On this section are three reservoirs, the largest of which covers about 100 acres, and is we believe, the second largest artificial reservoir in the county. One mile south of old Berthoud Mr. Welch owns 160 acres in section 22 of which 120 is sown. He also owns section 23 in the same township, of which 570 acres are in crop. Mr. Welch rents his farms on shares and speaks highly of all his tenants."

Frances Nielson, Helen Fickel, *The Heritage of Berthoud and the Little Thompson Valley*, Helen McCarty Fickel, Berthoud, Colorado, 1992.

Colorado Magazine, Vol. 25, #5 (Sept. 1948).

Berthoud Bulletin, Oct. 28, 1927.

1880 Precinct No. 8 (Little Thompson) census.

Fort Collins Courier, Feb. 13, 1879; Mar. 22 and Dec. 13, 1883; Jan. 17, 1884.

2.11   The Handy Ditch Company

In June 1877, *The Golden Transcript* reported, "A number of prominent citizens of Longmont are organizing a stock company for the purpose of building an irrigating canal, leading from the Big Thompson, that will irrigate all the land between that stream and the Little Thompson."

When the Longmont-Cheyenne Extension of the Colorado Central neared completion in October 1877, the *Denver Daily Times* added, "Not the least important factor in the success

Handy Dam on the Big Thompson River c. 1920. (Berthoud Historical Society)

of the line will be the ditch which is to be taken out between the Big and Little Thompson. The ditch will be taken out well up the [Big] Thompson and will run along the divide between the two creeks named, covering for the present about twenty-thousand acres—capable of supporting a thousand souls. Instead of being conducted in a flume along the precipitous hogback, the ditch will pass through the hogback by a tunnel. This will permit the watering of the land close up to the foothills and all along the line of the ditch are capacious natural reservoirs that will gradually fill up and insure a plentiful supply of water at all seasons. The land under it is being rapidly taken up and already claim shanties are dotting the landscape in every direction. Once put under cultivation this section will be one of the most prosperous in Colorado."

While the Longmont speculators established a charter for the ditch, they did not prepare to build it, offering instead to sell their franchise for $5,000. Meanwhile, a group of citizens from Golden hired Henry P. Handy to survey the course of a similar canal that would use a half-mile wooden flume to skirt a rocky hogback and run on higher ground.

In March of 1878 Charles C. Welch, John C. Hummel, Allison H. DeFrance and F.E. Everitt of Golden plus Lewis Cross of Berthoud formed the Handy Ditch Company in Golden. Ditch contractor J.A. Banning was hired to construct the canal. That spring Banning put 120 teams on the job estimated to cost $6,000.

Water began flowing though the Handy Ditch in 1881 after the canal and a high diversion dam at the mouth of the Big Thompson Canyon were completed. For two years, the wooden flume that skirted the hogback carried water from the river to the main canal. In 1883, a tunnel was constructed to replace the flume.

Peter Turner, who had a 160-acre homestead one mile north of Berthoud, supervised the tunnel's construction. Turner's son, William, later recalled, "When first constructed, the water ran in a flume from the present mouth or intake of the tunnel to the present outlet of the tunnel right around the point of the mountain. In one place there was a hanging flume suspended by rods from above. The result was that the thing was a failure for the first four or five years. Just as they would get to going well, the flume would break and down would go the water."

William Turner continued, "In 1881, Peter Turner made a survey of the tunnel on his own initiative and made an estimate of the cost of $15,000. He presented it to the board of directors for consideration, but the cost seemed so much that they laughed him out of it. But after another bad failure in 1882, on account of the flume's failing to function, they changed their minds. At the annual meeting they elected him a member of the board of directors and authorized him to let a contract for and

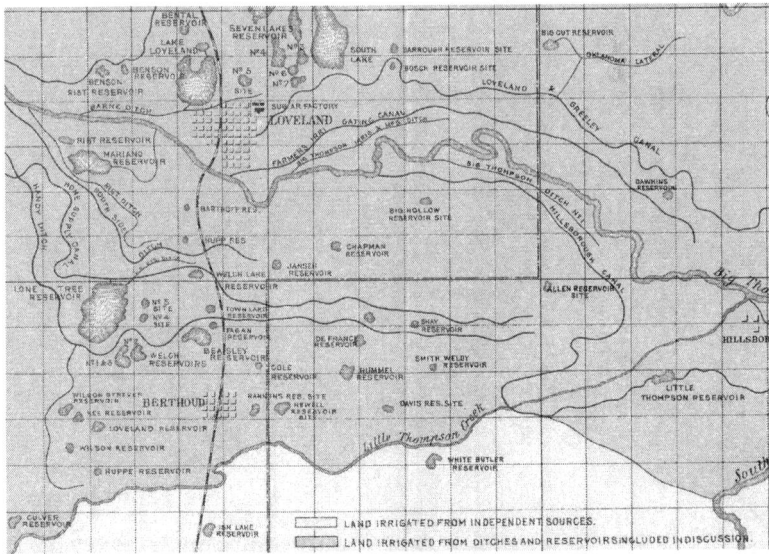

Handy Ditch and other southern Larimer County ditches and irrigation reservoirs. (U.S. Dept. of Agriculture, 1901) Note the names of many early settlers attached to various reservoirs: Culver, Ish, Huppe, Wilson, Loveland, Welch, Davis, Hummel, DeFrance, Hankins, Newell, Smith, etc. (Larger map at end of book)

to supervise the building of the tunnel. Among his old friends in the mining town [Sunshine] he found a contractor, a man by the name of Coon Apger, who tackled the job, and in due time the tunnel was completed.

"The tunnel would be drilled from both ends simultaneously, and Peter Turner scoffed at his critics that predicted the two headings would never meet. There may have been a bet involving a quart of whiskey on the outcome. Peter Turner's distracters said that the only way it would work is to drill straight through from one end. The two headings met perfectly."

A series of small lakes on the high ground between Berthoud and the Big Thompson Canyon were enlarged to serve as reservoirs for the Handy Ditch system. A sprawling network of ditches connected them, including Dry Creek, Loveland Lake & Ditch, Campion, McIntyre, Whipple and Sunnyside laterals. They were constructed to move water from the canal to farms lying north of the Little Thompson River. Peter Turner's homestead on the bluff above the Berthoud settlement was one of the farms served by the Handy Ditch.

North portal of the Handy Tunnel along West County Rd. 22H west of Loveland, Colorado. (Mark French)

In 1881-82, the Home Supply Ditch Co. constructed a log and rock-fill dam on the Big Thompson about three-quarters of a mile down river from the Handy Dam. The Home Supply Ditch Co. was organized to deliver water to a large area that included a section of the Little Thompson Valley south of Twin Mounds.

Note: The Home Supply log dam on the Big Thompson River washed out in 1894 and was replaced with a stone dam. The stone dam was damaged in the 2013 flood, but for the most part, remains standing today.

Golden Transcript, June 20, 1877.

Denver Daily Times, Oct. 22, 1877.

Boulder County News, Feb. 8, 1878.

Berthoud Bulletin, Feb. 26, 1931.

Reginald Keirnes, *Water: Colorado's Most Precious Asset*, Mile High Printing, Loveland, Colorado, 1986, pp. 4-6.

2.12 Gold Fever on the Little Thompson

In the winter of 1878-1879, there was a gold rush to the foot-hills of the Little Thompson. In January 1879, the *Fort Collins Courier* announced, "On Saturday last we made a visit to the new mines on the Little Thompson. Great excitement prevails and at least fifty men were there, all with fond hope of striking something. The town of Berthoud was represented by J.W. Everhard, John Ish, Lewis Cross and two of his sons. Headquarters seem to be at David Lykens <sic>. Judge Owens, of Boulder, was on the docket. Mr. Lykens <sic> conducted a party of us to his claim about a mile above his ranch on the

Little Thompson. Mr. Lykens <sic> is an old California miner of '49 but after all his experience he says that over this discovery he is non plussed. He & Co. have taken the above claim of fifteen hundred feet square. The lead is some five or six feet in thickness and above the ore is found a covering of decomposed mineral matter which resembles chalk... We also visited Wildcat mine in Wildcat Gulch owned by H. Kruger and Chas. Meining. Some of the ore looks well but as yet nothing definite is known as to the richness of it, until the assay is made by Mr. Hill, which will be done this week."

In February, the Little Thompson gold rush came crashing to an end. The *Denver Daily Tribune* reported, "In a conversation with Judge Owen <sic>, who has been investigating the Little Thompson excitement, we learn that the thing is a fraud. He says that Holland and Crocker of Longmont, made an assay, giving $8,991 per ton. A piece of identical rock assayed by Lawrence Thompson of Boulder, gave a trace of gold and one ounce in silver. The excitement was undoubtedly gotten up by some Longmont fellows, by way of diversion, as a relief from the monotony of pitching quoits and whiskey."

John Ish, a member of the Berthoud party that surveyed Lykins's claim, never lost his interest in gold. In 1881, Ish went on a summer prospecting expedition while his wife remained behind to oversee the harvest. In 1883, Ish staked a mining claim on Jack Creek in Teller County. Along with John W. Everhard, Ish also mined in Grand County where he developed the Lizzie and Highlander claims in 1884. In the late 1880s, Ish left the Little Thompson Valley for North Park where he followed his mining and cattle ranching interests.

Fort Collins Courier, Jan. 30, 1879; July 12, 1883; Oct. 23, 1884.

Denver Daily Tribune, Feb. 4, 1879.

2.13 Last Cattle Roundup

By the spring of 1879, the tracks of the Colorado Central Railroad were in place. The reservoirs and canals of the Boulder and Larimer County Irrigating and Manufacturing Company and the Handy Ditch Company had taken shape. The open range, where cattle had grazed since the 1860s, was vanishing with the construction of roads and fences.

William Turner, who was 11 years old at the time of the last big cattle round-up in the Little Thompson Valley later recalled:

The latter part of May 1879, after a day spent fishing on the Little Thompson, I was returning home by way of Uncle Lewis Cross's ranch when I was noticed and called into the house by Aunt Susan Cross...In the course of her conversation, while I was eating my lunch, she informed me that the roundup would camp for the night at the Cross ranch. As I had never seen a roundup I was all ears while she explained that there would be eight or ten mess wagons and from 50 to 100 men in the crowd... They had rounded up that day at the 'Big Barn' Wolaver ranch, and were slated for Lone Tree the next day. As it was all new to me and very exciting, I got permission from my father to use one of our work horses for the next day.

The men started from camp, the Cross ranch, in bunches of twos, threes or fours. The ones having the farthest to go started first, and drove every hoof of cattle that was west of the railroad, south of the Big Thompson, north of the Little Thompson and east of Chimney Hollow and rounded them up in the basin of what is now Lone Tree Lake by 10 or 11 a.m. All the boys were in and the routine work of the roundup began.

The whole thing was systematized; every man seemed to know just what to do and just how to do it. They ate their dinners in relays. Half of the men ate while the other half kept the cattle in order... By 4 o'clock they were through and ready to move to the next roundup. Those men were in the saddles or on their feet continuously from daylight until dark, about the longest days in the year, about 16 hours.

William H. Turner, *Berthoud Bulletin*, June 23, 1932.

2.14 1880 Census of Little Thompson Precinct

William Turner concluded his account of the last cattle drive in the Little Thompson Valley by noting, "By the middle of the next summer [1880] all of the big herds were out of the country, and the beginning of the eighties brought an influx of settlers who brought a new life and energy to the straggling community."

The 1880 Larimer County census of "Little Thompson" con-
firmed Turner's observation. In June of that year, households
headed by farmers and stockmen included those of Chalmon
Wray, Arthur Beeson, John C. Shull, Samuel W. Cole, Adam
Alkire, Warren Blinn, Cyrus D. Farwell, Alonzo D. Bassett,
Edward W. Day, Henry Alvin Huppe, Charles R. Meining, James
M. Coombs, Adolph H. Krueger,
David Dapp, John W. Everhard,
John S. Ish, John Kerr, Stephen
G. Preffer, John J. Preffer, Elijah
Randall, Lewis Cross, Simon
B. Bennett, Samuel Caywood,
Stephen S. Osborne, William S.
Flora, and William Snively.

Another class of workers
identified by the 1880 census was lime burners. Austen
Gleghorne of Indiana and
Zachariah and Matthew Carter
of Kentucky were identified as
such. Lime, a key ingredient in

Simon B. Bennett
(Berthoud Historical Society)

plaster, whitewash and mortar, was produced by burning lime-
stone in pits or kilns. A ready supply of this rock was available
in the foothills west of Berthoud where the Carters established
their homesteads. Zachariah and Matthew Carter are the namesakes of present-day Carter Lake Reservoir.

William Osborn and Richard A. Connell were listed as
clergy. A large number of men like Herman and Hugo Huppe
were farm laborers. The occupation of every adult woman was
"keeping house."

The census also revealed that in 1880, Berthoud amounted
to little more than a cluster of buildings on the Cross homestead
as well as the log school-house, the Colorado Central depot, and
the Colorado Central section house.

Individuals who could have been considered residents of Berthoud in 1880 were Lewis and Susanna Cross, both of whom were in their early sixties, and their sons Benjamin (32-year-old farmer), Dillon (26-year-old miner), and William (20-year-old stockman). Included in the census was a boarder with paralysis, 46-year-old Jefferson Carwile. He lived with the Cross family in their new home. Jeff Carwile may have been the former toll bridge operator, William J. Carwile, who with his brother, Oliver W. Carwile, relinquished the homestead claim taken up by Lewis Cross in 1873.

Colorado Central Railroad section boss John McCormick and his 22-year-old sister Bridget were among five people who made their home in the section house at that time. Bridget worked as the housekeeper while John O'Hern and John Ward worked as section hands. All were natives of Ireland. James Murphy, a farm laborer, also lived there.

Station agent Leonard H. Kelly resided by himself in an undisclosed location. It is certain, however, that in 1881 Kelly got married in Cheyenne and moved his bride, Debbie Emma Huntsman, to a house he'd built in Berthoud.

The 1880 census also identified a member of the John Ish household, 19-year-old Albert S. Thompson, as a "clerk in store." Thompson's place of employment may have been the store of James Piatt. In 1878, Piatt opened a store in the building where Lewis Cross operated the Little Thompson Post Office. Piatt's name did not appear on the 1880 census.

William H. Turner, *Berthoud Bulletin*, June 23, 1932.

1880 Census of Little Thompson Precinct No. 8.

Fort Collins Courier, June 16, 1881.

Berthoud Bulletin, May 3, 1934.

2.15 Train Wreck on the Colorado Central

In 1881, the lives of the community's residents revolved around the Colorado Central Railroad which threaded its way through the tiny settlement of Berthoud. For that reason, a train wreck that occurred south of Berthoud in July of that year caught everyone's attention. Even homesteader Davis Baxter, who seldom penned more than a few words in his journal, took time to note, "train rected <sic> on the C.C."

A few days later the *Denver Times* reported, "Yesterday evening train No. 2 left for Denver about half past seven, expecting to reach the city about two o'clock this morning. The worst known places in the road had been safely passed over and the train was mounting the grade between Longmont and Berthoud station about half past eleven o'clock last night. It had just reached the summit of a hill, where no danger was expected in the least, when suddenly, without warning, the engine plunged down into a culvert, over which the bridge had been washed away. The engineer, Frank Whitney, was instantly killed, and the fireman, W. Tillery, pretty badly injured.

"The engine had fallen upon the pilot and the baggage car breaking its couplings shot right over the tender. On the front platform of the baggage car, a tramp was stealing a ride, and

Steam-powered locomotives such as this one used by the Colorado Central in 1884 had difficulty ascending the grade out of Berthoud when the settlement was located on the Little Thompson River Bottom. (Mark French Collection)

when the accident occurred, he was hurled beneath the wreck and instantly killed. Baggage master Cree was badly bruised and cut, and the mail agent LaCourse received a serious shaking up, but no injuries were sustained. None of the other passenger cars of the train, or any of the passengers were hurt."

For years the tracks of the Colorado Central were damaged by unforgiving weather in the deep cuts through the bluffs north and south of the Little Thompson river bottom. In each cut, dust from nearby fields drifted over the tracks during windstorms and rain washed ballast from beneath the tracks during downpours.

The Longmont-Cheyenne Extension had been built with such haste in 1877 that along some stretches of the line, track was laid on mounds of dirt rather than crushed rock or ballast. That may have been the case in the cuts through the bluffs above the Little Thompson where horrific train accidents claimed lives in 1881 and 1890.

Denver Times, July 25, 1881.

2.16   The Journals of Davis Baxter

One of the most informative first-hand accounts of early Berthoud and the activities of the homesteaders living on the farms surrounding the town comes from journals penned by Davis Johnston Baxter from 1880 to 1886. Baxter, whose farm was on the Larimer-Weld County line one mile east of the Berthoud settlement, was among the first wave of homesteaders who staked claims in the Little Thompson Valley in the late 1870s.

Baxter was born in Ohio in 1847. Three days after turning 17, he enlisted in Company C, 2nd Ohio Volunteers Heavy Infantry and went off to fight with the Union in the Civil War. He served to the end of the conflict in 1865.

Davis J. Baxter (1847-1908) grave marker at Greenlawn Cemetery, Berthoud, Colorado. (Mark French)

In 1872, Baxter, his wife Susan, and baby daughter Agnes came to the Colorado Territory where they farmed near present-day Niwot. Baxter moved his small family to the Little Thompson Valley in 1874 where he staked a 150-acre homestead claim. Baxter's mother and sister filed tree claims on adjoining parcels that they relinquished to him later.

Baxter's early years in the valley were marked by the loss of his wife and two children. In 1881, he married his second wife, Martha Tope. In January 1884, he was among a group of local homesteaders who obtained land for Berthoud's cemetery. Two years later in January 1886, Baxter's son by his first wife, Sammy, died. Rather than bury him in the new cemetery, Baxter laid him to rest in the Burlington Cemetery near Longmont where his first wife, daughter, and mother were already buried.

More work than woe was recorded in Baxter's journals. Each page was filled with one-line entries recording the dates of his farming activities such as constructing a reservoir and digging irrigation ditches, harvesting ice in the winter for use in summer, and smoking a wolf out of its den to protect his livestock. Baxter also wrote about gathering cuttings from cottonwood trees on the Little Thompson river bottom to plant on his mother's and sister's tree claims.

In December 1882 for instance, Baxter logged: "9—fixed the house; 10—at church; 11—holled <sic> wheat to Berthoud; 12—helped D.O. Osborn thrash; 13—killed 2 hogs wate <sic> 432 lbs; 14—went to Loveland; 15—fetched calf paid Dan Osborn $10 dollars." Baxter skipped making entries for two weeks but concluded the month by writing, "28—Mother was sick; 29—baby was born."

In later years Baxter was among the founders of the Christian Church in Berthoud. He was also known for being "commander" of Decoration Day activities in Berthoud in the early 1900s.

Frances Nielson, Helen Fickel, *The Heritage of Berthoud and the Little Thompson Valley*, Helen McCarty Fickel, Berthoud, Colorado, 1992.

Unpublished journals of Davis Baxter: 1880-1886.

"Burlington Cemetery." *Longmont Heritage*, Vol. 6, No. 4 (Nov. 1994).

Berthoud Bulletin, June 3, 1905.

2.17 New Brick School Building

In June 1882, the Board of School District No. 22 called a special election "...for the purpose of voting on a school house site and creating a bonded indebtedness sufficient to build a school house." The measure passed and the decade-long era of the log cabin school came to an end. When the new school was completed, the cabin that had been constructed in 1873 was moved to a farm a few miles away.

Following the election, Secretary John Y. Munson advertised for bids in the *Loveland Reporter* and *Longmont Ledger*.

Munson also presented a contract to Mr. R.H. Hammond to teach at the Dist. No. 22 school from September through December at a salary of $55 per month.

In July 1882, a school census identified potential students between the ages of six and 21 years. A total of 31 students were found within the families of Samuel Caywood, W.H. Davis, John Everhard, John Kerr, Walter Finton <sic>, John Ish, John Munson, Elijah Randall, John Ullery and the Morrison, Marshall, and McNown families. Not all 31 enrolled but their vacant seats in the old log cabin school were filled by children from the Davis Baxter, John Clark, Thomas O'Brien, John McCormick, and Peter Turner families.

Preparations for the construction of the new school began in November 1882. Judge Marvin Delos Whipple, who had a homestead a few miles northeast of Berthoud, was paid $2.50 to survey the school site. School bonds were printed at a cost of $30. Contractor John Colpits of Longmont was selected to construct the brick school building at a cost of $1,451.50.

In February 1883, when the building neared completion, the *Fort Collins Courier* reported, "Billy Montgomery, carpenter, and Stevenson & Milne, plasterers, who went to Berthoud,

Larimer County District No. 22 School at Berthoud. (Alan Peacock)

Tuesday, to finish the school house, returned last evening. The interior was completed except the painting of three blackboards, but the weather barred any outside painting. The school house is a model of neatness and convenience." Before the school opened for classes in March 1883, an additional $103.50 was spent on modern desks.

Now equipped with a train depot, post office, blacksmith shop, general store and a new brick school building, Berthoud found itself poised to become the agricultural center of southern Larimer County.

Larimer County School Dist. No. 22 records.

Fort Collins Courier, Feb. 8, 1883.

2.18   Baseball on the River Bottom

While there were only a small number of people living in Berthoud in 1883, there were still enough young men in the community to field a baseball team. At that time nearly every town in the region, no matter how small, had a club to represent the community and provide recreation for players and spectators.

The first published mention of a baseball team in Berthoud occurred on May 3, 1883, when the *Loveland Reporter* noted in its "Berthoud News" column that a "A base ball club has been formed with several experienced players in the organization."

On May 17, 1883, the newspaper identified the team as the Berthoud

Hawks. That summer the Hawks competed with clubs from Fort Collins, Loveland and Highlandlake.

William Turner identified Hiram Maize as a member of Berthoud's first baseball team. In a tribute to Maize in the 1933 *Berthoud Bulletin*, Turner wrote, "Hiram Maize, an old timer of Berthoud and a colorful character was born somewhere in Missouri about the year 1860, but in the spring of 1881 he concluded to go west and grow up with the country and headed for what was then Little Thompson...He was a great big man about 6 feet 4 inches, a ruddy complexion, red hair and a red mustache; stood straight up and was about as fine a looking specimen of a man as it would be possible to see.

"He soon found employment, going to work first for Mr. Ish, a rancher just west of the Little Thompson station. He proved to be a good worker, was both affable and intelligent. In short time he knew everybody in the neighborhood and everybody knew him, and he was soon taking part in about all of the activities of the neighborhood.

"Mr. Maize was a fine fiddler and prompter, and taught many of the buck-a-roos, including myself, how to call figures and changes for a quadrille...He was an active member of the first baseball team ever organized here, the Old Berthoud Blues. He at one time owned one of the finest driving teams in northern Colorado, a pair of fine strawberry roans, Oregon horses. He also owned a race horse which was raced all over the northern part of the state under the name of 'Old Hicks.' But after he married, which I think was about 1886 or 1887, his habits changed, as he devoted all his time to raising and educating his family."

Loveland Reporter, May 3, June 21, and July 12, 1883.

Fort Collins Courier, May 10, 1883.

Berthoud Bulletin, Mar. 23, 1933.

2.19   New Bridge for Berthoud

In the spring of 1883, the Larimer County Commissioners decided to erect a new iron bridge over the Little Thompson River at Berthoud. In May, a contract for $604.25 was awarded to the Canton Iron Bridge Company for the bridge structure. The firm of Blair & Co. from Loveland was hired to construct the stone abutments and complete excavation at 25 cents per cubic yard of material. The bridge was completed later that summer.

On June 28, 1883, the *Fort Collins Courier* noted, "This structure will prove of much benefit to Berthoud." The newspaper acknowledged that the new bridge was on the main road through southern Larimer County and the fledgling town of Berthoud had much to gain from the heavy horse and wagon traffic that passed through on its way to points south.

Original stone abutments for the iron bridge constructed at Old Berthoud in 1883. The flood of September 2013 swept away a modern bridge that had replaced it. The bridge was located on Larimer County Rd. 15A one mile south of present-day Berthoud. (Mark French)

Fort Collins Courier, Apr. 12, May 10, and June 28, 1883.

2.20 Berthoud on the River Bottom: 1877-1883

The growth of Berthoud began in 1877 when the Colorado Central Railroad completed the Longmont-Cheyenne Extension and set a boxcar near the tracks to serve as its depot. By 1880, a section house had been added to serve as living quarters for the Section No. 13 section boss and small crew that maintained that segment of the rail line. The homestead cabin of Lewis Cross, another log cabin that doubled as a church and schoolhouse, corrals and a barn used as a stage stop were already in place when the Colorado Central arrived.

In January 1879, the *Fort Collins Courier* announced that Lewis Cross had built a fine brick residence. Later that month the newspaper added, "The growth of this quiet village [Berthoud] seems slow but sure. Mr. Cross, our postmaster, is just finishing his house...The schoolmaster, Mr. Harris [Jesse], now occupies the 'log cabin in the lane,' formerly occupied by Mr. Cross."

Lewis Cross house (left), iron bridge over Little Thompson River (center) and Colorado Central Railroad section house (right) at Old Berthoud. (c. 1915, Berthoud Historical Society)

In June 1881, the *Fort Collins Courier* reported that men by the names of Snyder and Grill had constructed a two-story store building in Berthoud. The tabloid also announced that Colorado Central depot agent Leonard Kelly had built a comfortable house. Pappy Fenton also built a blacksmith shop and house in 1881. Sometime earlier, Cross apparently platted a town site in order to sell building lots. The fate of the plat document is unknown, but an 1884 property transaction shows the settlement sat on a 270- by 400-foot parcel north of the Cross home.

The mercantile business operated by Snyder & Grill was purchased by John Y. Munson of Longmont in 1882. In August of that year the *Loveland Reporter's* correspondent noted, "Munson & Co. are doing a lively trade in dry goods and groceries...Our village blacksmith [Fenton] has more work than he can do...Evans and O'Brian [Colorado Central Section No. 13 section boss] have each added to the growth of Berthoud by erecting a large tent on opposite sides of the Main street, which affords a commodious shade for dogs by day and a cool place for a weary man at night...We have a Sabbath school and preaching every Sunday but I am sorry to say that they are held in the little old cabin instead of being in a good brick or stone house."

In 1883, Lewis Cross gifted a small parcel of land on the south bank of the river to District No. 22 for the site of a new schoolhouse. By March of that year the school was ready for students. In April, the *Fort Collins Courier* announced that Cross was "...putting up a house in town to be occupied by Mr. Frank Smith." Mr. Smith was the clerk at the Munson & Co. store. In the summer of 1883, Larimer County also erected a new iron bridge at Berthoud to span the Little Thompson River.

February 1883, found Samuel Pye, "sawing out lumber for parties to build a flouring mill here in the spring," according to the *Loveland Reporter.* By that year the Colorado Central had constructed a small frame depot building to replace the boxcar that had served that purpose since 1877.

The fledgling town was poised for growth in the spring of 1883. In March the *Fort Collins Courier* reported, "A large flouring mill that will do merchant and custom work is an enterprise much talked of. Two different firms are figuring on the cost, etc. and are casting about for a suitable location. One or the other will surely build the present season. The railroad company has already offered ground alongside the switch, which will be driven by steam, and will be first class in every particular, containing all the modern improvements for the manufacture of high grade flour. Messers. Caywood [Samuel Caywood] and Mullen [John Kernan Mullen] will also build adjoining the proposed mill a large elevator for storing and handling grain. These two enterprises will be of vast importance to the prosperity of the Little Thompson Valley as well as convenience to the people of that rich agricultural section."

In May 1883, reporter J.G. Ridgley of the *Courier* added, "On the Little Thompson creek <sic>, at the southern edge of the county, instead of the half-dozen settlers of former times, there is now a strong farming community stretching up and down and out on either hand, where but a few years ago we rode the prairie at will among the antelope. Now our way is hemmed by straight lanes that stretch and fade in their long way between rich farms. At Berthoud is already the beginning of a thrifty village."

That month Ridgley also lamented, "No point north of Denver offers better inducements for a general store; also a flouring mill is better needed. There is but one store here."

The *Loveland Reporter* noted in May 1883 that "A new carriage company has opened out in Berthoud, who deal in carriages only." The newspaper added, "Miss Alice Lincoln, of Longmont, appears in town twice each week to give music lessons."

Due to the absence of a "regular contributor," there was no Berthoud news recorded in the *Fort Collins Courier* from July 1883 through October 1883. The *Loveland Reporter*, however, continued its occasional coverage and reported in July that "Munson & Co. are preparing to build a large granary near the C.C. track."

In its "Berthoud Notes" of August 1883, the *Reporter* added, "Bartholf & Johnson have their grain warehouse nearly completed...Friday evening there is to be a social hop in Johnson & Bartholf's elevator." Frank Bartholf and H.E. Johnson were Loveland businessmen.

The following week the Loveland newspaper offered a recap of the dance when it noted, "Bartholf & Johnson's elevator was dedicated by about 40 ladies and gentlemen who tripped the light fantastic to the excellent music furnished by J.J. Preffer and B. Turner on Tuesday of last week." John J. Preffer and Beverly Turner were members of homesteading families that lived nearby.

The first indication that the thriving town of Berthoud might be moving from its original site on the Little Thompson river bottom appeared in the *Loveland Reporter* on August 30, 1883. On that date the tabloid announced: "Peter Turner of Berthoud made us a pleasant call last Saturday. From him we learn that the C.C. road has made arrangements to erect a new, commodious and substantial depot building on Pete's land just west of his house."

On September 20, 1883, the Loveland newspaper added, "P. Turner and S.M. Caywood are putting in a pair of scales at the new switch one mile north of the town." For that venture Turner, the homesteader upon whose property the new switch was located, partnered with Sam Caywood, a local wheat farmer and grain dealer.

In November 1883, the *Fort Collins Courier* announced that Turner had platted a new town site for Berthoud on his farm one mile north of the original settlement.

Residents of the Little Thompson Valley have long been told that the original town site proved unsuitable to the Colorado

Central because their steam-powered locomotives struggled to ascend the grade from the river bottom after stopping at Berthoud to take on loads. At the end of the 1883 harvest season, for instance, it was estimated that 100 to 150 carloads of grain were shipped from Berthoud's river bottom depot.

A new depot and switch on higher ground provided a solution to the problem.

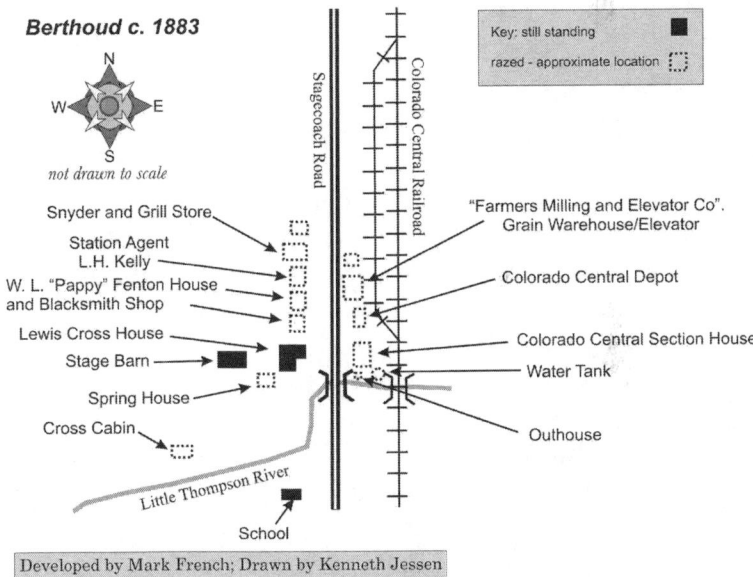

Note: Buildings and building sites of the original Berthoud town site on the Little Thompson river bottom, c. 1883, as estimated by author Mark French.

Fort Collins Courier, Jan. 30, 1879; Mar. 22, Apr. 19, May 3, May 10, Aug. 23, and Dec. 13, 1883.

Frances Nielson, Helen Fickel, *The Heritage of Berthoud and the Little Thompson Valley*, Helen McCarty Fickel, Berthoud, Colorado, 1992.

Loveland Reporter, Feb.1, May 3, Aug. 2, Aug. 16, and Aug. 30, 1883.

2.21   Turner Plats a Town Site

On November 27, 1883, Peter Turner traveled to the Larimer County seat in Fort Collins to file a "Platte <sic> of the Town of Berthoud." The new town site was located at the southeast corner of the 160-acre homestead Turner had claimed in 1878. Turner had proved up on the farm one month earlier in October 1883. Turner's farm, watered by the Handy Ditch, was located on the bluff one mile north of the Little Thompson river bottom.

Turner filed the plat two days after the *Fort Collins Courier* announced, "Mr. Peter Turner, proprietor of the new town of Berthoud, which has just been laid out on the hill one mile north of the Little Thompson creek <sic>, came over Tuesday to file a plot of the city. The town is laid out on section 14 of township 4, range 69, and lies principally on the west side of the railroad, and is fast filling up. Eleven building lots are contracted for, by persons who intend to build on them."

The building at 315 Mountain Avenue was relocated from the original town site to present-day Berthoud in the winter of 1883-84. (Photo c. 1910) The frame structure sat east of the railroads tracks before being moved to its current location. In 2016 the building was repurposed by the City Star Brewing Company to serve as its "barrel room." (Berthoud Historical Society)

Giving the town a new name was discussed. The *Courier* noted earlier that a Loveland grocery store owner planned to build a store in the new town of Turnerville. The new name, however, did not materialize and Berthoud carried most of its buildings—and its old name—to its new site on the bluff above the river bottom.

Fort Collins Courier, Nov. 22 and Nov. 29, 1883.

2.22 Goodbye to the River Bottom

By December 1883, Berthoud was starting to settle into its new footprint on the bluff above the Little Thompson river bottom. K.R. Golden, who had a livery and freight business in Longmont, began the process of relocating the town when he moved the first house to the new town site.

Nearly all the buildings in old Berthoud, with the exception of the new District No. 22 schoolhouse and the house and barns of Lewis Cross, had been moved by February 1884. That month the *Fort Collins Courier* reported, "We found the old town [Berthoud] almost deserted as the stores, warehouse, etc. had all been removed to the new town site about one mile north of the former location. The present situation of the place is far superior to the old one it being accessible by good roads from all parts of that section of the country as well as affording an excellent shipping locality...The rail company will probably soon remove their depot to the new place, as at present the shipping business is carried on with great disadvantage on the account of the distance between the town and the agent's office. Preparations are being made for the removal of the post office, Father Cross having already received the necessary permit from the government and it will be but a short time until the old town of Berthoud will be entirely wiped out."

It is likely there were no more than a dozen buildings in Berthoud, but most were lifted from their foundations, lowered onto wooden beams, and wheeled to the top of the bluff. One of the buildings was the Colorado Central depot. Others included Pappy Fenton's house and blacksmith shop and the store building owned by Munson & Company. A warehouse operated by Frank Crane was also relocated to the new town. (In 1897, the *Berthoud Bulletin* reported that Crane and J.K. Mullen had previously conducted business in the warehouse at old Berthoud under the name of the Farmers' Milling & Elevator Co.) Another building that was moved was the house Lewis Cross built for Frank Smith. The large frame building was purchased by J.C. Shull and used as a boarding house in the new town. The house constructed by depot agent Kelly remained at the old town site for at least a few more years.

At the time of the town's relocation, Berthoud was thriving on the Little Thompson river bottom. In 1883, the construction of a new brick school house was underway, the installation of a sturdy iron bridge spanning the Little Thompson had been completed, a grain warehouse had been built, and the addition of other improvements such as a granary and flouring mill were being contemplated. Yet the Colorado Central Railroad built a new switch on level ground one mile north of the town.

The Colorado Central Railroad was well aware that its steam-powered locomotives struggled to ascend the grade out of the river bottom after taking on loads of grain at Berthoud. Railroad company executives, particularly W.A.H. Loveland and Charles C. Welch, also knew that the recently-constructed Handy Ditch system could deliver water to the level ground lying on the bluff above Berthoud and that it was no longer necessary for the company's steam engines to stop at the Little Thompson River to replenish their tanks with water.

Access to the original town site had also been hampered by a patchwork of roads and the sizable dirt embankment that carried the tracks of the Colorado Central across the wide river bottom. It was also apparent that the embankment limited the town's expansion and restricted the area available for the construction of rail sidings needed for granaries and a flour mill.

Since none of these problems existed at Peter Turner's new town site, Berthoud was moved from the river bottom to the bluff in the winter of 1883-84. There was no appreciable resistance.

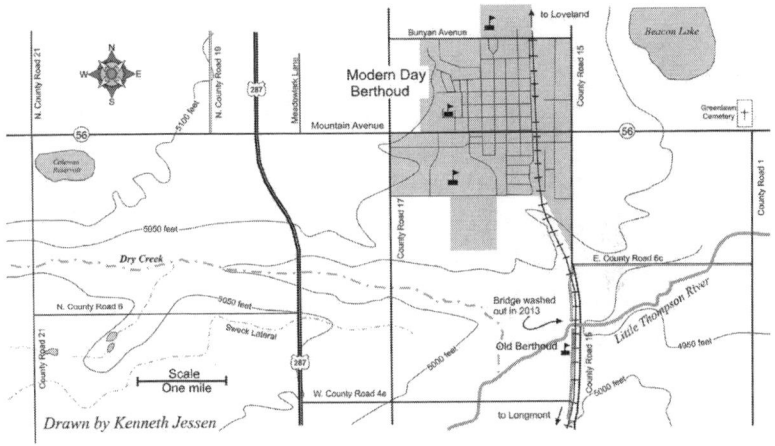

The original Berthoud settlement, identified as "Old Berthoud" was moved to "Modern Day Berthoud" in the winter of 1883-84. (Map by Kenneth Jessen; larger version at end of book)

Fort Collins Courier, Dec. 13, 1883; Feb. 7, 1884.

Berthoud Bulletin, Jan. 21, 1897; June 27, 1908.

Loveland Reporter, Mar. 13, 1884.

Frances Nielson, Helen Fickel, *The Heritage of Berthoud and the Little Thompson Valley*, Helen McCarty Fickel, Berthoud, Colorado, 1992.

2.23 Old Berthoud

After Berthoud moved to the bluff, residents of the community began referring to the site of the original settlement as Old Berthoud.

Even though most of the buildings were gone, the 1883 brick schoolhouse remained and served as a country school. By the following year, the school was known as the Old Berthoud School. It kept that name until 1954 when Berthoud's town and country schools were consolidated into one district.

As Berthoud came to life on the bluff, the vitality of the Cross family, like the settlement they had founded, began to fade. On January 19, 1884, while Berthoud was being moved from the river bottom, 31-year-old Ida Cross died of cancer. She was the daughter-in-law of Lewis Cross and the mother of two young children.

Cross, Marv Whipple, Davis Baxter, John W. Everhard, John Kerr, and Peter Turner quickly secured a site one mile east of the new town, established a cemetery, and buried Ida Cross there two days later.

Ida's daughters Ada and Bessie joined the household of their grandparents Lewis and Susanna Cross. Mrs. Cross fell dead 14 months later while sweeping her kitchen. Lewis Cross buried his wife in the family plot at the new cemetery.

After the passing of Susanna Cross, Ada and Bessie lived in the home of their uncle William. In July 1886, he died of pneumonia and in 1887, his wife died after a lengthy illness. An aunt, Sarah Cross Wilson, took the girls into her home near the foothills west of Berthoud. Both girls died from diphtheria in 1896.

Lewis Cross died on November 19, 1887. He was laid to rest in the cemetery he had helped establish three years earlier. Following his death, the *Fort Collins Courier* eulogized, "Early Sunday morning news was received in this city that Hon. Lewis

Cross of Berthoud was dead, the sad event occurring at 6:45 the evening previous at his son John's residence in Denver.

"His remains were brought to his late home at Berthoud for interment by Monday morning's train, and a large concourse of sorrowing relatives, friends and neighbors followed them to their last resting place. The funeral discourse was preached by Rev. W.H. McCormick of the United Brethren Church of which organization Mr. Cross had for many years been a beloved member.

"Mr. Cross's death was sudden and unexpected. He went to Denver on Thursday last to visit his son John who is engaged in business in that city, and was apparently in the enjoyment of his usual health. Shortly after breakfast Saturday morning he was stricken with paralysis, from the effects of which he never recovered.

"Lewis Cross was born May 10, 1816, in Rockingham County, Virginia, and was consequently 71 years old last May. He lived at the place of his birth until he was sixteen years old, when he emigrated, with his father's family, to Wayne County, Indiana,

Lewis Cross constructed this brick dwelling in the fledgling town of Berthoud in 1879 and lived there with his family until his death in 1887. The building still stands at the Old Berthoud town site. (Berthoud Historical Society)

where he followed farming. In 1840 he removed to Iowa, which was then known as the Far West. He came to Colorado in 1860, settling first at Central City, afterwards locating on Ralston creek, near the city of Golden, where he lived until 1873, when he moved his family to a farm in the Little Thompson Valley, one mile south of the present site of Berthoud.

"His life was one of usefulness and benefit to mankind. It cannot be said of him that the world is no better for his being in it. He filled many posts of honor and responsibility, executing every trust with fidelity. He was a specimen of God's grandest handiwork, an honest man. He served sixteen successive years as justice of the peace and soon after his arrival in the Little Thompson Valley was appointed postmaster, which office he held until domestic affliction and broken health admonished him to resign, which he did about a year ago. He was chosen county commissioner at the election held in October, 1876, serving one term and discharging the duties of his office with an eye single to the interests of the people. He filled the office of chairman of the board of county commissioners the last year of his term.

"No man in Larimer County was more widely known and no man more greatly revered and beloved by his fellow citizens than Lewis Cross. The memory of the many good deeds of this kindly old man and the teachings of his useful life are all that is left to us who remain behind. Let us cherish these and keep them fresh in our hearts by trying to emulate his examples."

Larimer County Genealogical Society. *Greenlawn Cemetery, Berthoud, Colorado,* 1992.

Davis Baxter journals.

Frances Nielson, Helen Fickel, *The Heritage of Berthoud and the Little Thompson Valley*, Helen McCarty Fickel, Berthoud, Colorado, 1992.

Fort Collins Courier, Nov. 24, 1887.

Berthoud Bulletin, Dec. 31, 1896.

PART 3

BERTHOUD
ON THE BLUFF

Town of Berthoud

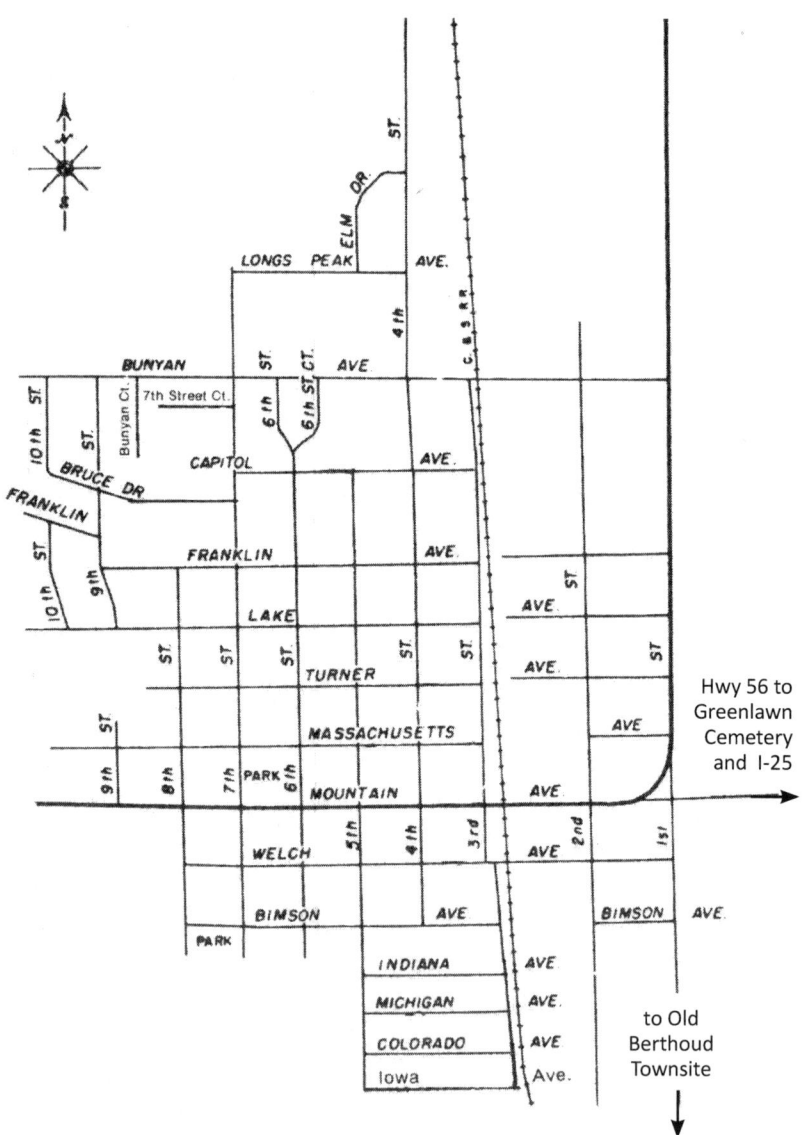

3.00 Turner's Town Plat

Berthoud's new town site consisted of an L-shaped grid of eight city blocks at the southeast corner of Peter Turner's 160-acre homestead. To the valley's early residents, that location was known as Turner's Corner. The town was situated where the Longmont-to-St. Louis Road intersected a pair of dusty ruts that led to the rural districts east and west of the new town site. The tracks of the Colorado Central Railroad sliced through the center of the proposed settlement.

The town had four east-west thoroughfares named Thompson, Welch, Munson, and Pine streets. Each measured 80 feet in width. Two of the streets' namesakes, Charles C. Welch and John Y. Munson, had ties to Old Berthoud: both backed moving the town away from the river bottom or the site Munson had called "down in the hole." Pine Street took its name from the region's ubiquitous conifer tree and Thompson Street honored the namesake of the Big Thompson and Little Thompson valleys.

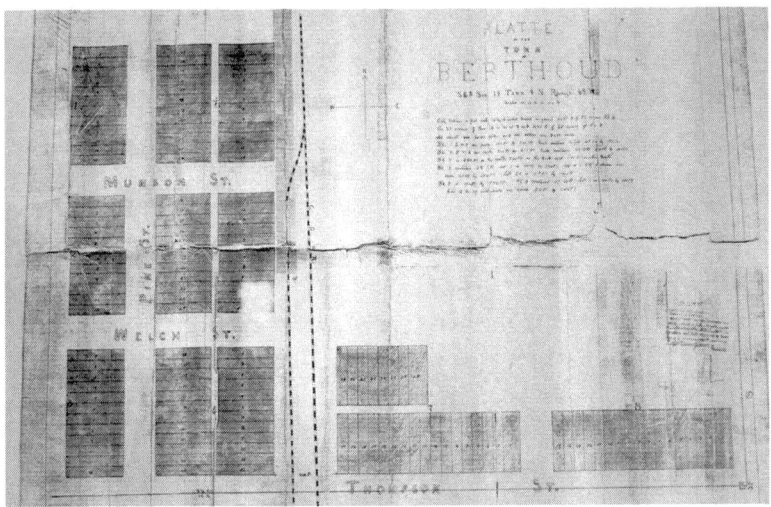

"Platte of the Town of Berthoud" filed by Peter Turner, November 1883.

Turner's plat had 150 building lots. Each lot was 25 feet wide and 140 feet deep, with the exception of the lot where Turner's 1877 homestead house stood. Turner's lot at the northwest corner of the present-day intersection of 1st Street and Mountain Avenue was an extra 15 feet in width.

A few days after Turner filed the town plat for Berthoud, the *Fort Collins Courier* reported that 11 building lots had been sold. Those prime lots, purchased mainly by businessmen, were located along an unnamed street that paralleled the tracks of the Colorado Central. That busy thoroughfare became 3rd Street when the town's north-south streets were numerically identified in 1893.

Fort Collins Courier, Nov. 29, 1883.

Berthoud Bulletin, Mar. 2, 1899.

3.01 Peter Turner

Peter Turner, the man who platted a new town site for Berthoud, was born in Virginia in 1838. He immigrated to Iowa in 1857 and farmed there until 1861 when he followed the gold rush to the Colorado Territory. Turner returned to Iowa three years later where he married Elizabeth "Betty" Searcy and resumed farming. In 1872, the lure of his earlier discoveries in the Sunshine mining district, the Hawkeye and Golden Eagle lodes, pulled him back to the mountains west of Boulder.

In 1874, Turner's wife and sons, Beverly and William, joined him at the Sunshine mining camp. There, Turner staked claims on two profitable mines—the Emancipation and the Old Dominion. A daughter, Susan "Susie" Sunshine Turner, was born into the family while they lived in Sunshine.

Concerns with his wife's health prompted Turner to relocate his family in 1877. He astutely selected a quarter-section of land in the Little Thompson Valley that would be on the path of the Colorado Central Railroad between Longmont and Cheyenne. His homestead claim was one mile north of the 1873 Lewis Cross farm on the Little Thompson river bottom. Turner's homestead house was one of the first dwellings to be built on the high ground between the Big and Little Thompson rivers.

Peter Turner (seated center) and family. (Berthoud Historical Society)

After improving his homestead, Turner helped develop the Handy Ditch that brought irrigation water from the Big Thompson River to the northern slopes of the Little Thompson Valley. In 1883-84, Turner supervised the boring of a tunnel through a rocky hogback at the mouth of the Big Thompson Canyon. Turner's tunnel replaced a rickety wooden flume and helped improve the Handy's ability to move water from the river into its extensive network of ditches and reservoirs.

In the summer of 1883, when the Colorado Central built a railroad switch on his land, Turner platted a new town site on his homestead one mile north of the original Berthoud settlement. In 1890 when Berthoud needed a hotel that measured up to those in other northern Colorado communities, Turner constructed the Turner House at the northeast corner of 4th Street and Massachusetts Avenue. The lodging house was renamed the Grandview Hotel in 1893.

Even though Turner and his sons lived in Berthoud, they maintained their remote mountain mining claims and prospected whenever possible. Turner's periodic visits to the Sunshine mining camp allowed him to cross paths with F. Irving Davis and John Hartford. At Turner's urging, Davis and Hartford moved their families to Berthoud where they opened one of the town's first hardware stores in 1886.

Peter Turner died in 1912 at the age of 74 years. He was buried in the family plot in Greenlawn Cemetery.

Frances Nielson, Helen Fickel, *The Heritage of Berthoud and the Little Thompson Valley*, Helen McCarty Fickel, Berthoud, Colorado, 1992.

Belva Turner Bashor, *Early Berthoud: A History of the Town 1877-1900*, The Old Army Press, Fort Collins, Colorado, 1976, p. 1.

3.02 Greenlawn Cemetery

Berthoud had just settled into its new footprint on the bluff when the death of Ida Cross prompted the community's leaders to establish a cemetery. Prior to her passing, Little Thompson Valley residents buried their loved ones in cemeteries located in neighboring communities such as Burlington (forerunner to present-day Longmont).

Ida, the daughter-in-law of Lewis Cross, lost her battle with cancer on January 19, 1884. Unprepared for such an event, Judge Marvin D. Whipple, Davis Baxter, Peter Turner, Lewis Cross, Major John Kerr and John W. Everhard scurried to locate a local site for a burial ground.

One day later, on January 20, 1884, a small parcel of land one mile east of the new town was secured for the cemetery. The following day, January 21, 1884, Ida Cross was laid to rest. United Brethren Reverend J.W. Zimmerman conducted her funeral service in the new school house at Old Berthoud.

Judge Whipple, namesake of the Whipple country school, gave the name "Greenlawn" to the cemetery.

Later, it came to light that Pete Turner and John Everhard had purchased the cemetery site at the southeast corner of Section 13, Township 4, Range 69, in Larimer County. Harrison Kindred Hankins, a farmer and a recent arrival from Iowa, was among the first citizens to buy burial plots. Hankins purchased ten plots for the total sum of $15.

Ida Cross marker at Greenlawn Cemetery. (Mark French)

Berthoud Bulletin, May 27, 1921.

Fort Collins Courier, Feb. 21, 1884.

Frances Nielson, Helen Fickel, *The Heritage of Berthoud and the Little Thompson Valley*, Helen McCarty Fickel, Berthoud, Colorado, 1992.

3.03   1884: Berthoud's First Year on the Bluff

Blacksmith W.L. "Pappy" Fenton moved his forge from the original settlement to the northeast corner of the present-day intersection of 4th Street and Mountain Avenue in 1884. (*Berthoud Bulletin*, Sept. 7, 1901)

Berthoud's move from the river bottom to the bluff got underway in November 1883 when Peter Turner began selling building lots. The town's transfer occurred swiftly because there were fewer than a dozen buildings to be moved and the distance between town sites was less than one mile.

All the buildings moved from Old Berthoud were frame structures lacking the modern conveniences of indoor plumbing and electricity. During that era buildings were moved by lifting them from their rock foundations with screw jacks, installing frameworks of heavy timbers beneath their floors, and attaching iron wheels mounted on axles to the timber framework. Teams of oxen or draft horses then towed buildings to their new sites.

In December 1883, barely two weeks after Turner filed his new town plat, the *Fort Collins Courier* announced that two Loveland businesses, A.A. Tuttle's hardware company and Bowman & Day's grocery, planned to establish branch stores at Berthoud. John Bowman of Bowman & Day was the acting mayor of Loveland. By the summer of 1884, Bowman had liquidated his Loveland interests and relocated to Berthoud. He quickly became one of the town's leading citizens.

Several Old Berthoud businesses moved to the new town. A warehouse for a grain brokerage firm operated by Frank Crane for Denver flour baron John K. Mullen was moved to an unknown location. John Munson built a new building at 549 3rd Street for the Munson & Company general store and he moved his original building from Old Berthoud to a lot a few doors north of his new building. Pappy Fenton located his house and blacksmith shop at the northeast corner of present-day 4th Street and Mountain Avenue.

Because the new town's appeal lay in its business potential, firms such as Loveland's Bowman & Day quickly snapped up prime lots in the 500 block of present-day 3rd Street. That thoroughfare, like all of the town's north-south streets, had not been assigned names or numbers on Turner's original plat even though the bustling street ran parallel to the Colorado Central tracks.

By January 1884, two stores and two blacksmith shops were operating at full blast in Berthoud. The stores were the Munson & Company mercantile and the Bowman & Day grocery. The blacksmiths were Pappy Fenton and a smithy named Mason.

In February 1884, Postmaster Cross moved the post office from Old Berthoud to the back of Munson's new store building.

By March John Calvin "Cal" Shull had purchased the Frank Smith house in Old Berthoud and moved it to the new town. Shull's wife Nancy operated a boarding house and restaurant in the building that had been relocated to the 500 block of present-day 3rd Street.

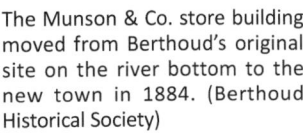

The Munson & Co. store building moved from Berthoud's original site on the river bottom to the new town in 1884. (Berthoud Historical Society)

The Barnes brothers, D.M. and W.O.R., constructed a frame building for use as a meat market and added an ice house with an eye to satisfying the town's appetite for ice cream the coming summer. Mrs. W.O.R. Barnes opened a millinery shop.

That month the Fort Collins newspaper also noted, "It is sadly remembered that a whiskey shop will soon be opened. There is a genuine, determined opposition to such a foul attempt. The sentiment of the good people has long been known inasmuch as a protest fully signed met a former attempt to open a dram shop."

The whiskey shop, operated by Pat Murphy, was located on the east side of the 600 block of present-day 3rd Street. When the building was finally razed in 1934, the *Berthoud Bulletin* recalled, "Generally speaking Murphy's saloon was an orderly place, but bullet holes in the walls and ceiling were reminders of at least one brawl in which there was gun play." By November 1884, Murphy was out of business, and Berthoud's fledgling Presbyterian congregation was holding revival meetings in the building.

In March 1884, the *Loveland Reporter* announced that a horse race had drawn a large crowd to Berthoud and that the "Longmont boys got away with the Lone Tree boys in the sum of about $150." The newspaper added, "Houses are very scarce now, not a vacant one can be found. Never in the history of the settling of the land between the two Thompsons were there so many plans prepared for farm houses of substantial character as are being drawn up at the present. Most prefer to build of brick and we understand the railroad depot will be built of that material, also the elevator; hence we fail to see why a well-managed brickyard would not pay being situated as near the timber here as any other small town along this line of the road."

When 1884 drew to a close, Berthoud was home to blacksmith shops operated by Pappy Fenton and Richard & Ehmensen. Both forges did brisk business shoeing horses, sharpening plows and attending to the needs of farmers who lived in the outlying rural districts. Daniel O. Osborn had opened a feed store equipped with a feed mill and corn sheller. Osborn had a set of whistles attached to the steam engine that powered his feed mill. He used the whistles to let farmers in the nearby countryside know he was producing fresh feed. Samuel Pye also erected a "feed and chop mill" that was up and running in March 1884. Samuel Caywood and Frank Crane operated grain handling businesses. At his warehouse, Crane sold grain, coal, and chickens raised in his "hennery."

Munson & Co. sold their store and stock of general merchandise to the firm Mahan & Rowan. Morgan & Morey, a branch of the C.S. Morey mercantile company of Denver, opened the town's second grocery store. W.S. Phipany of Loveland had also constructed two "business blocks" in Berthoud by year's end.

The fledgling town was also equipped with a drugstore that Fort Collins physician and druggist Dr. William W. Cole opened in the 500 block of 3rd Street. Billy Warren "flourished the

In 1884, the white frame building at the far right of the photo housed Pat Murphy's whiskey shop. By the time this photo was taken in 1903, Judge M.D. Whipple had purchased the building. (Berthoud Historical Society)

blade" in a barbershop next door to Cole's drug store. William
Mason and Sam Pye operated a meat market.

Mason, the butcher, built one of Berthoud's first houses
in April 1884. Charles R. Blackwell who was associated with
Bowman & Day, and Dan Osborn also built dwellings during

Ernest Newell (bottom left), Sid Davis (top right) and their families helped Berthoud
develop in the 1880s. (Berthoud Historical Society)

the town's first year. With 1885 on the horizon, there were nearly a dozen private residences in Berthoud.

With Berthoud on the rise, merchant John Munson began laying the groundwork for a bank. There was also discussion about building a schoolhouse in Berthoud since children living in the town attended the Mars Hill country school.

The need for a grain elevator was one of great urgency since dealers such as Frank Crane had found it necessary to stack sacks of grain in the open air until they could be shipped.

The town's first year ended with Colorado Central Railroad man Charles Welch making plans to plat an addition to Berthoud's southern boundary as one of many farms he owned in the Little Thompson Valley bordered the new town site.

Fort Collins Courier, Dec. 13, 1883; Jan. 10, 1884; Feb. 7, 1884; Mar. 5, 1884; Apr. 3, 1884; Nov. 20, 1884; Nov. 27, 1884; Apr. 16, 1885.

Frances Nielson, Helen Fickel, *The Heritage of Berthoud and the Little Thompson Valley,* Helen McCarty Fickel, Berthoud, Colorado, 1992.

Berthoud Bulletin, Aug. 2, 1934; Mar. 7, 1952.

Loveland Reporter, Mar. 5, 1884; Mar. 13, 1884.

3.04 Colorado Central Depot

In August 1883, the Colorado Central Railroad promised Peter Turner that "a new, commodious and substantial depot building" would be built on the land west of his house. Rather than fulfilling their promise the railway began shipping from both old and new Berthoud. It took several months to move the depot building from Old Berthoud to the new town. In February 1884, the *Fort Collins Courier* observed, "At present the shipping business is carried on with great disadvantage on the account of the distance between the town and the agent's office." At that time depot agent Len Kelly evidently still had his office in Old Berthoud.

The depot at Old Berthoud was finally moved to the new town in the summer of 1884. The small, frame building was placed a short distance south of the modern-day depot at the intersection of 3rd Street and Mountain Avenue.

The first shipment of grain from new Berthoud took place on August 18, 1884. At the end of that year, station agent Leonard Kelly reported that he had sold passenger tickets for a total value of $1,854.10. He also noted $3,712.56 had been collected for the shipment of freight.

Berthoud's first year at its new location (1884) saw the town emerge as the agricultural center of southern Larimer County. That year 277,361 bushels of wheat, 67,967 bushels of oats, 27,205 bushels of barley, 4,800 bushels of corn, 48,000 pounds of potatoes, and 24,000 pounds of pork were shipped from Berthoud by the Colorado Central. Of the wheat, 24,000 bushels (60 carloads) were sent to Chicago, St. Louis and Richmond, Virginia, where the grain was especially prized.

Berthoud depot, c. 1900. (Berthoud Historical Society)

Colorado Central rail service facilitated the movement of passengers and freight south toward Denver in the morning and back north later in the day.

Southbound passenger trains stopped at Berthoud at 7:41 a.m. and 2:22 p.m. while northbound trains picked up riders at 10:50 a.m. and 7:28 p.m. A southbound freight stopped in Berthoud for ten minutes at 10:40 a.m. and a northbound freight stopped at 2:02 p.m.

In 1886, the Colorado Central commenced construction of a new depot in Berthoud. The project straggled along for four years. Finally, in February 1890, the Fort Collins newspaper noted, "It is a beauty. For once the depot is a credit to the town."

The depot was built by Fort Collins contractor John G. Lunn. The north end was outfitted with living quarters for the station agent and his family. The old depot was moved to an unspecified location in Berthoud where it was used as a carpenter's shop before disappearing into oblivion.

Fort Collins Courier, Jan. 10, 1884; Feb. 7, 1884; Jan. 15, 1885; Jan. 22, 1885.

Fort Collins Weekly Courier, Aug. 26, 1886; Jan. 30, 1890.

3.05 Berthoud Farmers Alliance

A contentious relationship between Northern Colorado farmers and flour miller John Kernan Mullen, of J.K. Mullen & Co. in Denver, came to a head in 1883. That year Berthoud was still located at its original site on the Little Thompson river bottom.

In the fall of 1883, a large group of Larimer County farmers met in Fort Collins to explore the possibility of forming a Farmers Alliance. The formation of such an organization would enable them to pool resources and ship wheat to Chicago where wheat could be sold for six to 10 cents more per bushel than in Fort Collins. At that time area farmers sold wheat to Denver millers at prices up to $1.05 per hundredweight. Millers, including J.K. Mullen, ground the wheat into flour that sold for around $3 per hundredweight.

On December 1, 1883, a group of 30 wheat growers from the Cache la Poudre Valley voted to organize a Farmers Alliance and ship one carload of wheat to Chicago "...to be floured and thoroughly tested in eastern mills before making a general shipment of wheat."

In response, Mullen called a meeting of farmers, millers and threshers to be held in Longmont in January 1884. Mullen's milling firm, by far the largest in the state, was widely viewed as a monopoly that controlled the price of wheat.

Prior to Mullen's meeting, a group of 25 Berthoud farmers met at the schoolhouse in Old Berthoud to organize the Little Thompson Farmers Alliance. John Kerr was elected president and S. Wayland Cole as secretary. John W. Everhard and Cole were appointed to a shipping committee. The committee was given "...full power to receive and forward to eastern markets consignments of grain as should be made to them."

The Little Thompson farmers agreed to determine the amount of wheat that was still on hand in the valley. They also resolved to hold that wheat until it reached the price of $1.50 per hundredweight. Kerr reported that 32,000 bushels remained in local granaries. He added that 93,500 bushels of wheat had already been shipped from the Little Thompson Valley in 1883.

On January 10, 1884, over 100 Northern Colorado wheat farmers met with Mullen at the Dickens Opera House in Longmont to discuss the depressed condition of the wheat market. Mullen maintained that a surplus of wheat kept prices below $1.50 per hundredweight, a claim the farmers disputed. It was agreed, however, that a committee, made up of farmers

and millers would determine
the number of bushels of wheat
grown in 1883. They would
also determine the number of
bushels already ground into
flour and the number of bushels
required for home consump-
tion. Kerr represented Berthoud
on the committee.

A stalemate developed
between the farmers and the
millers. The wheat growers'
tally accounted for a shortage
of 150,000 bushels while the
millers' count identified a surplus of 150,000 bushels. Trusting
their calculations, the farmers resolved to band together to protect the price of wheat. By that time, branches of the Farmers
Alliance had also been formed by Greeley, Fort Collins,
Longmont, and Loveland area farmers.

Denver flour magnate John K. Mullen.

In February 1884, members of the Berthoud Farmers
Alliance (Little Thompson Farmers Alliance) reconvened at Old
Berthoud. A committee appointed to estimate the cost of building a grain elevator reported that $10,000 would be needed
to construct a 32- by 144-foot frame building with a capacity
of 100,000 bushels. Immediate action was not taken but work
began on articles of incorporation for an elevator and milling
company that would require a capital stock of $20,000 (800
shares valued at $25 per share).

In the spring 1885, Mullen beat the Berthoud Farmers
Alliance to the punch when he built the first grain elevator in
the new town and solved Berthoud's grain storage dilemma.

Fort Collins Courier, Nov. 22, 1883; Nov. 29, 1883; Dec. 6, 1883; Dec. 27, 1883;
Jan. 10, 1884; Jan. 17, 1884; Feb. 7, 1884; Sept. 11, 1884; Apr. 16, 1885.

3.06   J.K. Mullen's Elevator

During the town's first year, Frank Crane, an employee of J.K. Mullen & Co. of Denver, operated a grain business in Berthoud without the benefit of an elevator building. Since there was not an elevator in which to store grain, up to 5,000 bushels of wheat were piled in the open near the Colorado Central depot. That unsatisfactory arrangement ended in the spring of 1885 when J.K. Mullen & Co. built Berthoud's first grain elevator.

In April 1885, the *Fort Collins Courier* announced that a large force of workers had completed the massive stone foundation for the elevator and were prepared to put up plank walls.

In May, machinery was installed in the frame structure that rose to a height of 75 feet. The elevator was so impressive that the Fort Collins newspaper praised it as "...the most conspicuous object in all the valleys of the Thompsons."

Once completed, Mullen's grain elevator boasted a storage capacity of 80,000 bushels. The building was located along a rail siding on the east side of the Colorado Central railroad tracks about 150 feet north of present-day Mountain Avenue.

Fort Collins Courier, Jan. 15, 1885; Apr. 23, 1885; May 28, 1885; Oct. 25, 1888.

Berthoud Bulletin, Mar. 7, 1952.

3.07   Berthoud Waterworks

By the spring of 1885, it was clear that the town's water supply required urgent attention. During Berthoud's first year in its new location, town residents used wooden casks to haul water from the Little Thompson River or they dipped water from a murky pond east of the Colorado Central depot. The pond was filled with water drawn from Turner's Lake. The Handy Ditch filled Turner's Lake located a short distance northwest of town. That shallow lake no longer exists. It was, however, the namesake of Berthoud's Lake Avenue.

In April 1885, the *Fort Collins Courier* poked fun at Berthoud's water dilemma. The tabloid jested that water from the Little Thompson River was made up of "...95 percent pure water, 2 percent Epsom salts, 1 percent lime and 2 percent Babbit's Best Soda." The newspaper also teased that water from Turner's Lake was "...93 percent water, 1 percent frog spittle, 2 percent extract of polliwog flavored with muskrat, traces of guano and red water lice, 1 percent typhoid fever and 3 percent Lydia Pinkham's Vegetable Compound."

Andrew Fairbairn, who moved to Berthoud in 1887, later told the *Berthoud Bulletin* that, "...he and his family moved into town one forenoon, and that about 11 o'clock the cook stove was up and they began to think about the noon meal. He got a bucket and went out in search of water and was directed to a scooped-out place just west of the elevator, between the mainline of the railroad and the elevator track. He found a pool of stagnant water which he could dip from a plank or springboard which extended over the pool. With the bottom of the bucket he brushed away the green scum, bringing up a bucketful of slush which looked like anything but drinkable."

For a brief time there was speculation that an artesian well might be a possible source of Berthoud's water. That proposition was abandoned in the spring of 1887 when a stock company was organized to build a water system for the town. According to the *Fort Collins Courier*, three unidentified citizens each subscribed $1,000 to the enterprise that was estimated to cost $6,000.

In 1887, the stock company built a reservoir using water

drawn from the Handy Ditch about a mile and a half north of Berthoud. A pipeline was installed to carry water to town for domestic use and fire protection.

The Town of Berthoud purchased the waterworks from the stock company in 1889. At a meeting of the town trustees on July 9, 1889, water rates were established at $4 per building lot with an additional $3 fee to be paid for an adjoining lot. Additional adjoining lots carried a $2 fee per lot. Beginning in 1890, more water mains and fire hydrants were added to the system.

Fort Collins Courier, Apr. 30, 1885; Dec. 23, 1886.

Berthoud Bulletin, Oct. 26, 1933.

Belva Turner Bashor, *Early Berthoud: A History of the Town 1877-1900*. The Old Army Press, Fort Collins, Colorado, 1976, pp. 59-60.

3.08 Welch Addition Enlarges Berthoud in 1885

During Berthoud's first year, various enterprises were established in the booming town. In 1877, Charles C. Welch purchased the quarter-section that bordered the southern boundary of the town site Peter Turner platted in 1883. Welch bought the 160-acre parcel from the Denver Pacific Railroad & Telegraph Co. for $560. There were rumblings that he planned to plat an addition to the town.

Sure enough, in October 1885, Charles C. Welch filed a plat for the Welch Addition to Berthoud. The *Fort Collins Courier* proclaimed, "C.C. Welch has just laid out an addition to the town of Berthoud, south of and along the road running west from P. Turner's corner. Mr. Welch manifests a more liberal policy in the price and size of his lots than has prevailed heretofore, and as the location is, on many accounts more desirable than where the town is started, it is now thought that it will be the future center of business."

On November 20, 1885, Welch sold lots 1 & 2 in Block 3, Welch Addition for $175 per lot. Merchants Charles Blackwell and James Piatt purchased the prime property at the southwest cor-

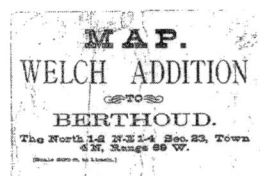

ner of present-day 3rd Street and Mountain Avenue.

With the opening of the Welch Addition, Thompson Street (present-day Mountain Avenue) became the town's main east-west thoroughfare. Business buildings and houses quickly filled this stretch of what eventually became the 200 and 300 blocks of Mountain Avenue.

Several months earlier, in April 1885, ground was broken for a brickyard west of the new town. It was expected that bricks produced there would supply a building boom anticipated to come that summer. Over 400 tons of stone for building projects, presumably from sandstone quarries located in the foothills west of town, also arrived in Berthoud that month.

For local entertainment, the Berthoud Band was organized by John Day of the Bowman & Day grocery store in May 1885. In its "Berthoud" column the *Fort Collins Courier* predicted, "On these beautiful early summer evenings the boys will make the denizens of this valley happy with their strains of melody."

For the sports-minded, the town's baseball team, the Berthoud Grays, was founded in August 1885, to compete with their rivals from Fort Collins. The Berthoud nine won the hotly contested game by a score of 11 to 10. The sons of blacksmith Pappy Fenton, Will and Frank, played catcher and left fielder for the Grays.

Berthoud's first lodge organization, the International Order of Good Templars (I.O.G.T.), was organized in the fall of 1885. Berthoud Lodge I.O.G.T. No. 37 met at the Mars Hill and Old

Berthoud country schools. Men and women were members of the temperance organization modeled after Freemasonry.

Berthoud's United Brethren church also earned headlines in the *Fort Collins Courier* in September 1885. That month it was announced that building lots had been secured and that $800 was in hand for the first church building to be erected in Berthoud.

Fort Collins Courier, Apr. 23, 1885; July 23, 1885; Sept. 3, 1885; Oct. 8, 1885; Dec. 31, 1885; Feb. 25, 1886; May 17, 1888.

The Berthoud Bulletin, Oct. 26, 1933.

Frances Nielson, Helen Fickel, *The Heritage of Berthoud and the Little Thompson Valley*, Helen McCarty Fickel, Berthoud, Colorado, 1992.

3.09 Bank Corner

Berthoud's first banking enterprise was established in July 1885. Longmont's Charles and Frank Stickney, cousins who were erroneously identified as brothers, and Sam Dobbins, who had been a business partner with John Munson at Old Berthoud, had interests in the bank. Dobbins rode the train from Longmont to Berthoud each day with money for the day's transactions.

It was not until the spring of 1886 that a building to house the bank was constructed. The first substantial stone structure built in the new town, the Bank of Berthoud was erected at the northwest corner of present-day 3rd Street and Mountain Avenue.

Preparations to construct the building began in February 1886. That month the Fort Collins newspaper reported that stone for the bank had been delivered to the building site. In August, the newspaper noted that work was progressing rapidly and that the new building would be "...an ornament to the town."

Work ceased in September when workers exhausted the supply of stone. Construction eventually resumed and by October 1886, the bank building was completed. Its location was at one of the town's busiest intersections and it soon became known as the "bank corner."

The Stickneys operated the Bank of Berthoud, serving the community until 1887. The bank closed its doors that year after Frank Stickney gave notice that "...the modicum of business was insufficient." Stickney withdrew to Longmont where he later became the President of the Farmers National Bank.

It wasn't until 1892 that another bank came to Berthoud.

Bank of Berthoud building. (Berthoud Historical Society)

Fort Collins Courier, Aug. 26, 1886; Sept. 16, 1886.

Berthoud Bulletin, Aug. 2, 1934.

Frances Nielson, Helen Fickel, *The Heritage of Berthoud and the Little Thompson Valley*, Helen McCarty Fickel, Berthoud, Colorado, 1992.

3.10 Prospects for a Flour Mill

In February 1886, the price of wheat plummeted even as farmers lamented a lack of winter moisture that made their fields too dry to plow. Although crop prospects for the coming summer were bleak, farmers assembled to discuss the possibility of building a flour mill. Their view was that the construction of a farmer-owned-and-operated flour mill would enable them to counter the monopoly of flour baron J.K. Mullen. Enthusiasm ran high at the meeting and a committee was organized to seek pledges.

Following the harvest in August, wheat prices plunged further to 63 cents per bushel. In spite of the low price paid for wheat, many area farmers sold to Mullen's Colorado Milling & Elevator Co. to get cash in their pockets. Mullen's company was so busy that an extra crew was hired to work at night.

Berthoud's businesses revived during the annual harvest season. The *Berthoud Beacon* noticed the bustle and observed, "Quite a number of farmers near town are threshing this week and when the threshers come in town toward evening our streets present a lively scene."

Lovejoy threshing outfit in front of Alfred Bimson's stone blacksmith shop in Berthoud, Colorado, c. 1897. (A.G. Bimson)

By December 1886, wheat was in short supply. Frank Crane, the manager of Mullen's elevator in Berthoud, increased the price paid to farmers to $1.05 per hundredweight. Local wheat growers who had the means to hold their wheat sold it in December, taking advantage of the higher price.

Fort Collins Courier, Feb. 25, 1886; Aug. 26, 1886; Dec. 23, 1886.

3.11   The *Berthoud Beacon*

The town's first newspaper, the *Berthoud Beacon*, began publication in August 1886. That month, the *Fort Collins Courier* began citing the *Beacon* as its source for Berthoud news. Prior to that time, the *Courier* obtained information about the new town through unnamed correspondents. Unfortunately, little is known about the *Beacon's* first editor, L.A. "Andy" Thompson.

On August 12, 1886, the *Courier* credited the *Beacon* for its description of Berthoud. The account noted, "Since the first of July we have started a meat market, commenced work on a bank that is to be a fine building for any town, built additions to two houses and are about to resume work on a church. Our streets are crowded every day with teams and our merchants are rushed with business. We support four churches. We have a lodge of Good Templars in a flourishing condition. Two Sunday schools look after the moral training of the young. No liquor is sold or given away within our borders. Take us altogether, we are a dandy little town."

The *Beacon* announced that meals were available at Jenny Shull's restaurant at a cost of 25 cents and that Henry Corcoran guaranteed his work as a mason and plasterer. Other Berthoud businessmen who advertised in the *Beacon* were blacksmith and wagon maker W.M. Richardson, and J.W. Dolloff, who sold fancy groceries.

The *Berthoud Beacon* ceased publication in November 1886. The *Courier's* last report from the *Beacon* announced that a new newspaper would soon be started in Berthoud. The account from the *Beacon* wryly noted that the newspaper's stock of a paste pot, two ink bottles and four lead pencils was for sale. Wishes for a mild winter were also extended to the next newspaper editor in hopes that he "...would not be compelled to freeze to death while rustling for grub."

Fort Collins Courier, Aug. 12, 1886; Sept. 2, 1886; Nov. 18, 1886.

Berthoud Bulletin, Aug. 2, 1934.

3.12 First Church Building Built in Berthoud

Berthoud's United Brethren congregation continued to meet at the school in Old Berthoud until 1886. During the town's first years, the Presbyterians worshipped in a building that had once housed a saloon in the 600 block of 3rd Street. A Seventh Day Adventist congregation, established by the Bestle family, met at the Red Rock school west of Berthoud. Other country schools around Berthoud were intermittent meeting places for various denominations ministered by traveling pastors.

While meeting at the Old Berthoud school in 1885, Berthoud's United Brethren shared its minister, Reverend H.J. Van Auden, with a sister congregation at Mt. Zion. A rural community with a church building, Mt. Zion was located between Highlandlake and Longmont.

By the fall of 1885, Van Auden had raised $800 for the construction of a United Brethren church building in Berthoud. Peter Turner helped forward the project by donating lots for the new church building at the northeast corner of present-day 4th Street and Turner Avenue.

On May 20, 1886, Reverend A.E. Seibert was appointed to Berthoud's United Brethren pastorate. Siebert had once been employed as the editor of the *Loveland Reporter* newspaper. In the following months, Seibert supervised the construction

The United Brethren church at the northeast corner of the present-day intersection of 4th Street and Turner Avenue in Berthoud was built in 1886. (Berthoud Historical Society)

of a brick church that had capacity for 200 souls. The church was completed in December 1886 and formally dedicated on January 2, 1887.

Even though the United Brethren built a church in Berthoud in 1886, the congregation continued to share Rev. Seibert with Mt. Zion until May 31, 1888. After that arrangement ended, a full-time minister was appointed to the Berthoud church.

Fort Collins Courier, Sept. 3, 1885; Oct. 7, 1886; Dec. 30, 1886; June 16, 1887.

3.13 Growing Pains

When 1886 came to a close, Berthoud had been at its new town site for nearly three years. That year, F. Irving Davis and John F. Hartford came to Berthoud from the Sunshine mining camp to open the Davis & Hartford general store. Their store was located in a frame building at the northwest corner of present-day 3rd Street and Massachusetts Avenue.

Charles R. Blackwell, an employee at the Bowman & Day grocery store, also arrived in 1886. Davis and Blackwell built homes at 549 and 521 4th Street respectively. John H. McCormick, who had been the Colorado Central section boss at Old Berthoud, erected a brick house on his homestead one-half mile east of the new town.

By year's end, Nancy Jane "Jenny" Shull had closed the hotel and boarding house she had opened in 1884. She continued to conduct a small café associated with the hotel. Shull and her husband John C. Shull made their home in a building behind their boarding house at 523 3rd Street. Mr. Shull operated a livery business in a barn he had built at 321 Mountain Avenue in October 1885. In 1886, Mrs. W.O.R. Barnes closed her millinery shop and a new barber had assumed the tonsorial duties of Billy Warren.

That year there was a report of a gambling house and an "infestation" of drunken bums in Berthoud. The following February, Stewart Sawdy was bound over to a grand jury "...for running the lowest kind of dive in Berthoud for some time, to the great detriment of society and the ruination of boys."

John C. Shull (*Berthoud Bulletin*, September 9, 1921)

J.W. Dolloff and William Dycer established a small lumberyard on the south side of East Mountain Avenue near the Colorado Central railroad tracks. The Dolloff & Dycer lumberyard was sold to Fairbairn & Hankins in 1887. The business was purchased by the Davis & Hartford Mercantile Co. a year later. Andrew Fairbairn managed the lumberyard for Davis & Hartford and became a partner in the business in 1892 when the business was enlarged and incorporated under the name of the Fairbairn-Davis Lumber & Coal Co.

The livery barn built by John Shull at present-day 321 Mountain Avenue in Berthoud in 1885 was later purchased by Simpson Jefferes and operated as the City Star Barn. Photo c. 1915. (Berthoud Historical Society)

Andrew Fairbairn (*Berthoud Bulletin*, July 22, 1921)

In the fall of 1886, *Berthoud Beacon* editor L.A. "Andy" Thompson observed the town's lack of amenities. Thompson wrote, "A few accommodations—a hotel, church, schoolhouse, a few trees, etc.—would help Berthoud out wonderfully. The business here is bound to support a good town, and the main point now is to make it a desirable place to live."

Thompson also took a poke at Peter Turner and Charles Welch, the men who owned most of the building lots in town. Thompson opined, "As we have said before, town lots in Berthoud are held at too high prices. We hope some of the property owners here will soon become far-sighted enough to know that it would be to their own interests to come down on them."

The year 1886 ended with Berthoud boasting about its new bank and church but mourning the lack of a school for its children and clean water for its residents. At the end of December, the *Fort Collins Courier* expressed surprise that there wasn't a school in a town the size of Berthoud. The tabloid speculated, "The reason seems to be that the inhabitants of this promising town are working at cross purposes. The line of the school district runs through the southern edge of the town and the districts on each side are bonded for school houses already built, and should the town lay out a district for itself, it would have to pay its proportion of the bonds in each of the other districts while receiving no benefits from the schools. However, our friends of Berthoud cannot afford to be without schools, let the cost be what it may."

As 1887 approached, there was optimism that Berthoud's citizens would finally have a modern water supply. The *Courier* confirmed that aspiration when it reported, "The people of

Berthoud will put in a system of water works this coming spring. They will organize a stock company for the purpose, and the work will be done by private subscription. It is proposed to build a reservoir on the line of the Handy Ditch, about a mile and one-third from town. This will give them a fall of a little upwards of eighty feet in this distance, which will create ample pressure for all purposes. The water will be taken from the highest ditch on the Big Thompson, so that there will be no seepage from other ditches in it. The estimated cost of this system is only $6,000, and three of the enterprising citizens of the place have subscribed $1,000 each to the enterprise. The people of Berthoud are very fortunate in being able to secure good water at so small an outlay, and they will find that by putting in this system they will be reimbursed many times by the increase in the value of property, besides it will be a paying investment for stockholders."

Fort Collins Courier, Sept. 2, 1886; Sept. 16, 1886; Sept. 29, 1886; Nov. 18, 1886; Dec. 23, 1886; Dec. 30, 1886; Feb. 24, 1887; Jan. 31, 1889.

Berthoud Bulletin, Jan. 28, 1897.

3.14 Murder at Red Rock

On a pleasant Sunday morning in August 1887, there was a shooting at the Ferguson & Hallett ranch in the Red Rock district two and one-half miles west of Berthoud.

The previous evening, George Martin, one of five or six hands employed at the ranch, had quarreled with another cowboy named Childers. When the men were getting up the next morning, the dispute flared up again and Martin fired his revolver at Childers. The bullet passed through Childers's shirt, grazing his chest, and struck a fellow ranch hand named

W.F. Greenstreet. Dr. W.W. Cole was summoned from Berthoud but all the physician could do to relieve Greenstreet's suffering was to administer an opiate. Greenstreet expired an hour after the physician's arrival.

Even though several ranch hands were present when the shooting occurred, they stood by while Martin packed his belongings, loaded his revolvers, and walked away toward the foothills. Later that day a telegraph was sent to Fort Collins to summon Larimer County Sheriff Ephraim Love. By the time a train delivered Love to Berthoud, Martin had a twelve-hour head start. With the assistance of a deputy, Sheriff Love scoured the foothills west of Berthoud. The only clue the lawmen uncovered came from a woman who had seen a man fitting Martin's description running through her field.

To aid in his apprehension, the Fort Collins newspaper described Martin as, "...five feet and five or six inches in height, and weighing from 140 to 150 pounds. Light complexion, hair light and clipped close, mustache clipped short. He wore dark clothes, a soft, light colored hat, and heavy shoes. His legs between the knees are remarkably short, which gives him a peculiar appearance. Nothing is known of his history as he came to this country only a short time ago."

Love and the deputy failed to capture Martin that night. The next morning they discovered that Martin had a bank account in Longmont containing $110. Love placed a hold on the account and located the photograph negative of Martin taken at a Longmont studio. Wanted posters were printed and posted over a wide area. Two months later George Martin was arrested in Fairfield, Iowa. He was returned to Fort Collins by Sheriff Love where he was tried and found guilty of manslaughter. Martin was sentenced to two years in the Colorado State Penitentiary.

Fort Collins Courier, Aug. 11, 1887; Nov. 3, 1887.

3.15   Dr. W.W. Cole

Dr. William W. Cole was the first physician to practice in the Berthoud community. A few months after the town was moved from the Little Thompson river bottom, the 34-year-old Cole relocated his family and medical practice from Fort Collins to the new town. Upon his departure, the *Courier* commended Cole as "...one of the best read physicians in Northern Colorado... a scholarly gentlemen of unswerving integrity and excellent social qualities."

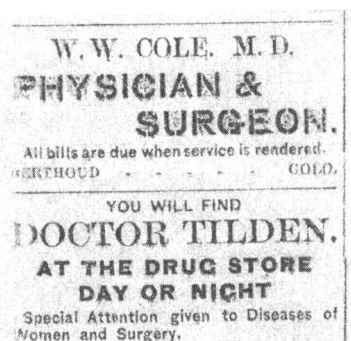

W. W. COLE. M. D.
PHYSICIAN &
SURGEON.
All bills are due when service is rendered.
BERTHOUD - - - - COLO.

YOU WILL FIND
DOCTOR TILDEN.
AT THE DRUG STORE
DAY OR NIGHT
Special Attention given to Diseases of Women and Surgery.

Dr. W.W. Cole and Dr. L.C. Tilden maintained medical practices in Berthoud during the town's first decade. (*Berthoud Blade*, April 22, 1892)

Years later, Belva Turner Bashor, the granddaughter of town founder Peter Turner, provided her perspective of Dr. Cole when she wrote, "He was an honest fellow, didn't know too much about medicine, and was honest enough to say so. Often, very often, he would be puzzled over some illness and would say, 'Well, now, I'll have to go home and read up.'"

Dr. Cole was educated at Rush Medical College in Chicago, Illinois. In August 1884, he came from Fort Collins and opened a drug store and medical office in a small frame building at 553 3rd Street in Berthoud. Cole soon built one of the first houses in Berthoud at 527 4th Street. His neighbors in that block of 4th Street were Colorado Central station agent Len Kelly who lived at 541 and merchant F. Irving Davis who resided at 549.

As a young man, Cole was a teacher. In 1887, he unsuccessfully ran for the office of Larimer County Superintendent of Schools. That year he also served as Berthoud's Justice of the Peace.

In 1889, Cole became Berthoud's third postmaster, a successful nominee of Republican President Benjamin Harrison's administration. In that era, local postmasters had the authority to determine their post office locations. During Cole's term, he operated the Berthoud Post Office in his drug store at 553 3rd Street and employed Isa Fenton, daughter of blacksmith Pappy Fenton, as his assistant postmistress.

Dr. Cole practiced in Berthoud from 1884 to 1906. He then moved to Wyoming where he worked as a physician for a mining company. Cole later relocated to Denver where he died in 1921.

Fort Collins Courier, Aug. 7, 1884; Feb. 24, 1887; June 16, 1887.

Frances Nielson, Helen Fickel, *The Heritage of Berthoud and the Little Thompson Valley*, Helen McCarty Fickel, Berthoud, Colorado, 1992.

Berthoud Bulletin, Mar. 11, 1921.

3.16   New School is "...a fine addition to town"

Until 1887, children living north of present-day Mountain Avenue attended the Mars Hill country school located southwest of the present-day intersection of North 1st Street and West Larimer County Road 10E. Children living south of Mountain Avenue attended school at Old Berthoud. Both schools provided classes for first through eighth grades.

This arrangement ended in the fall of 1887 when Mars Hill students were moved to temporary quarters at the United Brethren Church at 348 Turner Avenue.

Ed C. Willis, the Mars Hill schoolmaster, presided over classes at the church. The children of town founder Peter Turner and businessman Cal Shull were among his students. Willis also served one term as Berthoud's Justice of the Peace and was manager of the town's first baseball team, the Berthoud Grays.

For a time, the District No. 13 School Board considered moving the Mars Hill schoolhouse to the town of Berthoud. Instead, a new building was constructed on lots purchased from Peter Turner at a cost of $175. The lots were located northeast of the present-day intersection of 6th Street and Mountain Avenue.

At the end of December 1887, the *Fort Collins Courier* announced that the new schoolhouse in Berthoud was nearing completion and would be opened in January 1888. The newspaper added that the two-story brick building had two classrooms each equipped with 64 seats. The *Courier* noted that the schoolhouse also had a library and coal room. The new school was described as "...a very fine addition to the town."

John Harbaugh, a Loveland contractor, completed the building's carpentry. James Lunn of Fort Collins did the brickwork and Berthoud's Henry Corcoran completed the plastering.

When the new school building was opened in January 1888, Miss Mary R. Bell, the teacher at the Whipple School, took over teaching duties for the remainder of the 1887-88 school year. The student body consisted of 40 students. Frank Newell replaced Miss Bell at Whipple.

With District No. 13 no longer needing the Mars Hill school-

Smoke wisps from the chimney of the school constructed on the east side of present-day 6th Street near Fickel Park in 1887. (Berthoud Historical Society)

The staff and student body of the Berthoud School, c. 1890. (Berthoud Historical Society)

house, the structure was moved to the newly-formed Summit District No. 54 three miles south of Loveland. The new district began operation in January 1888.

In 1896, the 1887 school was replaced with a new building across the street and in the center of present-day Fickel Park.

Fort Collins Courier, Sept. 15, 1887; Dec. 29, 1887.

Berthoud Bulletin, Aug. 17, 1923; Nov. 27, 1930.

Frances Nielson, Helen Fickel, *The Heritage of Berthoud and the Little Thompson Valley*, Helen McCarty Fickel, Berthoud, Colorado, 1992.

Loveland Reporter, Jan. 5, 1888.

3.17   Berthoud Farmers' Milling & Elevator Co.

The construction of a flour mill—a proposition first discussed by local farmers when Berthoud was still located on the river bottom—finally became a reality in January 1888. That month, with capital stock of $50,000, the Berthoud Farmers' Milling & Elevator Company was incorporated by John C. Hummel, Charles C. Welch, Peter Turner, William Clark and William T. Newell.

In March 1888, the Berthoud Farmers' Milling & Elevator Co. purchased the 80,000-bushel grain elevator built by John K. Mullen in 1885 for $14,000. Mullen's elevator, accessed by the rail siding built in 1883, sat east of the Colorado Central tracks and directly north of the site where the flour mill would be built later that year.

By June, the construction of the flour mill building was complete but the flour-making machinery had yet to be installed. Taking advantage of the temporarily vacant building, Berthoud's volunteer firemen held a dance there on the evening of the Fourth of July to dedicate the new mill.

The steam-powered machinery with the capability of processing 300 sacks of flour per day did not arrive until October 1888. Even then, it was not properly installed and operating until the end of the year.

The Berthoud Farmers' Milling & Elevator Co. facility was constructed at a cost of $52,000. Frank A. Crane, who had previously worked for John K. Mullen, was hired to act as the mill's first manager. John Thomas was employed as the first head miller. The stone bank building at the northwest corner of 3rd Street and Mountain Avenue had closed in 1887 and

The Berthoud Farmers' Milling & Elevator Company. (*Berthoud Blade*, April 22, 1892)

this became Thomas's home. The company's bookkeeper, Ellet McNeil, built one of the town's first houses at the northwest corner of 5th Street and Mountain Avenue. The original night miller was a man named Frazier. John R. Preston and Ben H. Sexton shared duties as day and night engineers.

The first board of directors included town founder Peter Turner, A. Henry Krueger, J.H. Frank, Charles H. Keirnes and William T. Newell. At the company's first annual stockholders' meeting on January 14, 1889, Manager Crane reported that the mill's profit for 1888 had been $2,500.62.

The first flour produced at the Berthoud mill was marketed under the name *Farmers Pride.* Later other brands, including *Crown Patent, Extra Fancy* and *Blue Ribbon*, were added to the line.

In 1889, the grain elevator purchased from Mullen was enlarged. It surprised no one when Mullen constructed a second elevator in Berthoud a few months later. Mullen's Rocky Mountain Elevator was located southwest of the intersection of Mountain Avenue and the Colorado Central tracks. The towering frame granary had a capacity of 30,000 to 35,000 bushels and was operated under the auspices of Mullen's Colorado Milling & Elevator Company.

In 1884, Mullen bullied the farmers of Northern Colorado by warning them he would shut down every mill they built north of Denver within five years. Mullen did not accomplish his threat but remained involved in Berthoud's grain industry for several decades.

Berthoud Bulletin, Jan. 24, 1903; Apr. 3, 1952; Apr. 17, 1952.

Fort Collins Courier, Mar. 1, 1888; Mar. 15, 1888; June 21, 1888; Oct. 25, 1888; Dec. 13, 1888; Jan. 17, 1889.

Loveland Reporter, July 12, 1888.

Leroy R. Hafen, *Colorado and Its People*, Vol. 2, Lewis Publishing Company, Inc., New York, New York, p. 576.

3.18 John Bowman

John A. Bowman was one of early Berthoud's leading citizens, and like many men who settled in the community, he was a veteran of the Civil War. Bowman served the Union in the 75th Ohio Infantry. Following the war, Bowman presided as Commander of Loveland's Grand Army of the Republic (GAR) Burnside Post. Like some other war veterans, Bowman maintained friendships with fellow citizens such as John C. Ish and John W. Everhard, who had fought on the side of the Confederacy.

Bowman came to Loveland in 1882 and operated a grocery store. He was elected mayor of the town, running on the Prohibition Party ticket. After Berthoud moved to its new site during the winter of 1883-84, Bowman sold his business interests in Loveland and moved to Berthoud. He ran the Bowman & Day grocery store on 3rd Street and built one of the town's first houses at the northwest corner of 4th Street and Massachusetts Avenue.

In 1885, the firm of Bowman & Day sold its stock of goods to Blackwell & Piatt. Bowman then pursued other interests including the Holstein-Friesian Cattle Co. of Berthoud. Along with Colorado Central depot agent Leonard Kelly and grain broker Frank Crane, Bowman owned a herd that included 47 purebred cows and two fine bulls.

Bowman, who had taught for 15 years in Ohio before coming to Colorado, served as Secretary of the District No. 13 school board. In 1887, he made an unsuccessful bid for the office of Larimer County Superintendent of Schools on the Prohibition Party ticket.

In June 1888, Bowman filed a petition with Larimer County for the incorporation of the town of Berthoud. Frank Crane, Matthew A. Rowan, Leonard Kelly and F. Irving Davis were appointed as election commissioners and instructed to call and conduct the town's first election.

Later that month, the poor health of Bowman's wife prompted him to move his family to North Carolina. Although Bowman never made his home in Berthoud again, he played a key role in the town's development during its first four years.

Fort Collins Courier, July 10, 1884; Sept. 3, 1885; June 16, 1887; Oct. 20, 1887; June 21, 1888; June 28, 1888.

Berthoud Bulletin, Mar. 7, 1952.

3.19 Berthoud Incorporates

In July 1886, the *Loveland Reporter* noted in its Berthoud column that, "A movement is on foot to incorporate the town. It seems that opinion is divided on the subject."

It was not until July 17, 1888, that Berthoud held its first election, and then 30 of the 31 eligible voters approved the town's incorporation. Two weeks later, Larimer County Clerk Clark Moore certified, "Said town, according to statutory classification, is to be classed and denominated an incorporated town." That accomplished, Berthoud prepared to establish its town government.

On September 10, 1888, a total of 38 Berthoud voters participated in a second election. They selected eight town officers to serve until the spring of 1889 when another election would be conducted. F. Irving Davis, John Yale Munson, Andrew Fairbairn, Frank A. Crane, Peter Turner, Matthew A. Rowan and Leonard H. Kelly were elected without opposition. Berthoud voters also ruled by a margin of 23 to 15 that licenses would not be issued for the sale of alcohol.

F. Irving Davis was named mayor. Unfortunately, the Davis & Hartford general store that Davis operated with his partner, John F. Hartford, burned down a few weeks later. The frame building had been located at the northwest corner of 3rd Street and Massachusetts Avenue.

In the weeks following the September 1888 election the town board hired Edward Sperry to act as town marshal and street supervisor.

Berthoud's first mayor, Franklin Irving Davis, was elected to that office in September 1888. (Berthoud Historical Society)

Prior to the town's incorporation, the only equipment available for fighting fires was a makeshift hose cart that consisted of a reel of garden hose mounted on a pair of buggy wheels. Motivated by the smoldering ruins of the Davis & Hartford store, a set of ledgers and a hose carriage for the town's volunteer hose team were among the Town's first purchases.

Loveland Reporter, July 15, 1886.

Fort Collins Courier, June 28, 1888; Aug. 23, 1888.

Berthoud Bulletin, Apr. 3, 1952.

Belva Turner Bashor, *Early Berthoud: A History of the Town 1877-1900*, The Old Army Press, Fort Collins, Colorado, 1976, p. 58-59.

3.20 Davis & Hartford Store Burns

A full line of general hardware was sold from the Davis & Hartford store that had been constructed in the spring of 1886. Berthoud's first great conflagration was the fire that destroyed the frame building during the last week of September 1888.

Following the fire, Irving Davis and John Hartford used $5,000 from an insurance claim to rebuild their business. In October 1888, the partners hired Donovan Brothers, a firm with branches in Longmont and Fort Collins, to erect a 25- by 50-foot brick store building and 16- by 60-foot brick warehouse.

By January 1889, the new store building had been stocked and was doing a lively business.

The Davis & Hartford store building at the corner of 3rd Street and Massachusetts Avenue, c. 1910. (Berthoud Historical Society)

Fort Collins Courier, Oct. 4, 1888; Oct. 25, 1888; Dec. 13, 1888; Jan. 17, 1889.

Berthoud Bulletin, Nov. 4, 1910.

3.21 Irving Davis and John Hartford

After Peter Turner moved his family from the mining town of Sunshine to the Little Thompson Valley in 1876, he maintained his mining claims and returned to Sunshine periodically to check their status.

At Sunshine, Turner became acquainted with Franklin Irving Davis of New Hampshire. Davis, known by his middle name Irving, had discovered three mining claims: the Aragain,

F. Irving Davis (seated right) with wife Ida and daughter, Imogene. (Berthoud Historical Society)

Golden Slipper and Grand Island. With his partner, John F. Hartford, Davis made a handsome profit.

Turner encouraged Davis to use his profits to relocate to the new town of Berthoud where a hardware store was sorely needed. Davis and Hartford took advantage of Turner's tip and in the spring of 1886, moved to Berthoud where they had a frame store building constructed at the northwest corner of 3rd Street and Massachusetts Avenue. Earlier, one of the town's blacksmith shops had been located at that prime site near the Colorado Central depot. The blacksmith shop was moved to another location to make way for the Davis & Hartford Mercantile Company.

After their arrival in Berthoud in 1886, Davis and his family moved into temporary living quarters on the second floor of the store building that John Munson had moved from Old Berthoud in the winter of 1883-84. Davis's family included his wife Ida and their children Nettie Belle, Sidney and Imogene. Sid and Imogene had been born at the Sunshine mining camp in 1883 and 1886, respectively.

Within a few years, Davis built an elegant, two-story Victorian dwelling at the southwest corner of 4th Street and Massachusetts Avenue (549 4th Street). Among his neighbors were depot agent Leonard Kelly, Dr. William W. Cole and shopkeeper Charles Blackwell.

John Frederick Hartford, Davis's business partner, was a native of Sweden who came of age in Minnesota. Hartford was a hotel worker there until the prospect of striking it rich lured him to the Sunshine mining district near Boulder, Colorado. After discovering gold, he relocated to Berthoud where with his wife Minnie, he built a fine brick house at the corner of 4th Street and Mountain Avenue (no longer standing).

When the 31-year-old Hartford died unexpectedly in August 1893, he left behind a pregnant wife and young sons Fred and Albert. A daughter, Helen, was born six months after his death.

Following Hartford's passing in 1893 the *Boulder Daily Camera* noted: "Mr. Hartford was one of the most prominent citizens of that city (Berthoud) being a late partner of Davis & Hartford Mercantile Company. He owned some 1,900 acres of fine agricultural land near Berthoud and carried an insurance policy of about $25,000. Boulder people will remember him as one making such a rich strike in the Western Slope at Sunshine about eight years ago with his late partner, Mr. Davis."

After her husband's death, Minnie Hartford moved her family to Denver but returned to Berthoud several years later.

Irving Davis followed his former business partner in death in July of 1913. The Davis & Hartford store operated under various partners' names until its inventory was liquidated in the fall of 1922.

The F.I. Davis house at 549 4th Street in Berthoud. (Berthoud Historical Society)

Frances Nielson, Helen Fickel, *The Heritage of Berthoud and the Little Thompson Valley*, Helen McCarty Fickel, Berthoud, Colorado, 1992.

Boulder Daily Camera, Aug. 29, 1893.

3.22 Berthoud Hose Team

Berthoud's first hose company was organized in May 1888 when Justice of the Peace Ed Willis presided at a meeting held in "parlors over the post office." Willis was elected temporary chairman of a committee appointed to work on a constitution and bylaws and determine the cost of hose and a hose cart.

At a meeting in June 1888, M.A. Rowen was elected president; Willis, secretary; George Graham, foreman; Andy Fairbairn, assistant foreman; and H. Learey, second assistant foreman. It was also determined that the company would be out on parade and "be in good running order by July 4" when a "grand ball" was to be held at the Farmers' Mill.

Later, Belva Turner Bashor recalled, "On July 4, 1888, the Fire Department had their first dance in the new mill, dancing on the second floor. I was there, but only one month old...I've been told that it was a gala affair, enjoyed as only our pioneers

Berthoud Hose No. 1 (c. 1891, Berthoud Historical Society)

knew how to enjoy the few entertainments that came along. There was a capacity crowd and the musicians were from Longmont. They had two violins and an organ. One of the fiddlers, Mr. Mumford, called the square dances."

Berthoud Hose No. 1 hose house was located on the east side of the 500 block of 4th Street. (Berthoud Historical Society)

Berthoud Hose No. 1 was formally organized in August 1889. This fire-fighting company was equipped with a hose carriage that was purchased after the town's incorporation in July 1888. Members of this hose team were Andrew Fairbairn (foreman), Matt Rowan, Doc Searcy, John Munson, Ed Sperry, Harry Lovejoy, Charles Blackwell, Ben Sexton, Josh Barr, Bill Turner, Fred Richardson, Irving Davis and Jasper Pulliam.

In June 1890, a petition signed by 41 Berthoud voters led to the appropriation of $250 for the construction of a hose house. In July, a building committee was formed to procure plans for a frame structure that was also to contain the city jail. A dump (outhouse) and bell tower were added later that year. The cost of the hose house and various improvements totaled $324.20. The building also doubled as Berthoud's town hall.

Members of Berthoud's hose company were initiated prior to service. To test lung power, candidates were required to blow through a hose suspended from the hose house tower and force 25 pounds of water to the top. To test hearing, they stood erect while a stream of water at full pressure was directed at one ear. To prove their legs were in running condition, they were hung by their feet for five minutes.

On December 31, 1888, Berthoud's volunteer fire-fighters hosted their first annual New Year's Eve ball. The fundraising event was held on the second floor of the new Munson & Hubbell mercantile store at 565 3rd Street. Following the event the *Loveland Reporter* noted, "The firemen's dance came off Monday night and was largely attended. Everybody seemed to have a good time. There were euchre tables upstairs where those who did not dance could amuse themselves with that game."

The tradition of the firemen's ball continued into the early 1940s. The Turner Hotel and Mintener Hall, a large room on the second floor of the lumberyard on East Mountain Avenue, also served as locations for the event.

The Berthoud Hose Company in 1891, in front of Berthoud Farmers Milling & Elevator Company's buildings. (Berthoud Historical Society)

Loveland Reporter, May 26, 1888; June 16, 1888; Jan. 5, 1889.

Fort Collins Courier, Aug. 15, 1889.

Belva Turner Bashor, *Early Berthoud: A History of the Town 1877-1900*, The Old Army Press, Fort Collins, Colorado, 1976, p. 61.

Berthoud Bulletin, Aug. 18, 1900.

3.23 Death in the Clouds

Tragedy struck the Berthoud community in September 1889 when Frank Stryker lost his life on Longs Peak. The 23-year-old Iowan had been living with his uncle, Cornelius V. Stryker, who farmed east of Berthoud. During an outing on Longs Peak with his father and uncle, Stryker accidently shot himself with his 38 caliber revolver.

Carlisle Lamb, the son of Rev. Elkanah J. Lamb, was the party's guide. In 1877, the elder Lamb had been assigned to the United Brethren's Little Thompson Mission. Carlisle and Elkanah Lamb were considered to be the best mountain guides in the area.

In an article titled "Death in the Clouds," the *Fort Collins Courier* recounted, "...Frank carried a revolver in his hip pocket, and as it became cumbersome, he shifted it into a belt which he was wearing. He placed it just in front of his right hip, with the muzzle pointing upward, and started ahead of the party. In stepping from one ledge to another, he slipped and fell. In falling, the revolver was discharged and a large-sized bullet tore its way through his neck and windpipe making a horrible-looking wound from which his life-blood flowed in torrents.

"The injured man did not seem to realize that his wound was fatal and walked down the mountain about 200 yards, when he became exhausted and too weak to continue. He was laid on an improvised bed and the flow of blood was stopped. There was hope of saving his life and his friends anxiously awaited aid which young Lamb had gone for. As they had stayed in the mountains so long after the accident it was impossible to reach aid before dark and they kept up their lonely vigil on the verge of a precipice which was 1,000 feet above the deeps below.

"As it became darker they gave up hopes of succor before morning and tried to fix themselves as comfortable as possible. It began to grow colder and they were soon suffering from the chill mountain air. The clouds which had been gathering about the peak descended in a black pall which enshrouded them as a harbinger of death. To add to their torture snow began to fall and soon a winding sheet of pure white covered the mountain and the party. The shock to Frank's system caused by the shot and the intense cold was too much for his weakened condition, and with a fond farewell he died in the arms of his weeping father and uncle, who were nearly frantic with grief."

Frank Stryker's remains were removed from the mountain, taken to Longmont where they were placed in a metallic casket, and accompanied by his father to Iowa for burial.

In spite of numerous mishaps on the mountain, ascents of Longs Peak continued to be a popular pastime of Berthoud's early residents. With the towering Mt. Meeker on its southern flank, the majestic sentinel of Colorado's Northern Front Range possessed a magnetic appeal.

Longs Peak (right) viewed from Berthoud, Colorado. (Mark French)

Fort Collins Courier, Sept. 12, 1889.

Loveland Reporter, Sept. 5, 1889.

3.24 The 1889 Berthoud Business Boom

In 1889, Berthoud experienced a building boom that began to fill the lots in the town's small business district and residential neighborhood. In March, the *Loveland Reporter* observed "real estate is on the boom and corner lots are in active demand." Four months later the newspaper jested, "Town lots in Berthoud are so precious that a company of capitalists from Kansas are going to ship in four car loads next week."

That year, John Y. Munson hired Loveland contractor J.B. Harbaugh to construct a frame house at 105 Mountain Avenue. Harbaugh, a Larimer County Commissioner from 1883 to 1886, was responsible for building several homes in Berthoud around that time. Munson's business partner, Richard Montgomery Hubbell, also constructed a fine home at 444 1st Street in 1889. Hubbell's home, like Munson's, was equipped with modern conveniences such as a furnace and hot and cold running water.

The firm of Munson & Hubbell commenced the construction of a two-story, brick business building at 565 3rd Street in the summer of 1889. The building, completed in February 1890, was located at the same street intersection as the train depot and the Davis, Hartford & Co. store.

In 1889, Simpson "Sim" Jefferes, a farmer from the Red Rock district west of Berthoud, built a house at the southeast corner of 2nd Street and Mountain Avenue. (The dwelling is no longer standing.) A year earlier, Jefferes had purchased the Reynolds Livery Barn on East Mountain Avenue and re-named it the Star Livery Barn. In 1898, Jefferes sold the business and purchased the City Stables located on the south side of the 300 block of Mountain Avenue.

Jefferes and his family had been passing through Berthoud in 1886 when they camped for the night in the field east of Peter Turner's house. Mrs. Jefferes was ailing and Mrs. Turner cared for her. The Jefferes abandoned their plan to go to the Dakotas and started a new life in Berthoud.

In 1889, John and Nancy Shull added a dining hall to their hotel in the 500 block of 3rd Street. Rev. W.H. McCormick left the United Brethren ministry to homestead a farm two miles north of the new town. This same year, McCormick went into business with Ben Forbess. McCormick & Forbess ran a hardware store in an L-shaped building that wrapped around the bank at the corner of 3rd Street and Mountain Avenue. Their unique building had store fronts on each street.

The firm of Bennett & Orvis conducted a business in the building west of McCormick & Forbess on Mountain Avenue.

In 1889, Dr. R.J. Leggitt began the construction of a home at 609 5th Street. Leggitt moved into his new residence the following February. During his short stay in Berthoud, Leggitt practiced medicine and served as chief of Berthoud Hose Company No. 1. In 1890, Leggitt sold his home to W.H. McCormick, who moved there from his homestead north of Berthoud.

J.W. Turrell of Longmont erected a building in the 500 block of 3rd Street that year to house his drugstore. Turrell, who was also in business in Longmont, had expanded to Berthoud the previous year.

Another business to open in 1889 was Lutener Bros., also of Longmont. The Lutener brothers opened a wagon repair and paint shop on East Mountain Avenue. Samuel D. Lutener, the older brother, was a blacksmith. The younger brother, John M. Lutener, was a painter and carpenter who built several homes in the community.

Loveland Reporter, Mar. 11, 1889; July 25, 1889.

Fort Collins Express, Jan. 1, 1894.

Fort Collins Courier, June 21, 1888; Mar. 28, 1889; May 16, 1889; June 6, 1889; Aug. 15, 1889; Oct. 17, 1889; Feb. 6, 1890.

Frances Nielson, Helen Fickel, *The Heritage of Berthoud and the Little Thompson Valley*, Helen McCarty Fickel, Berthoud, Colorado, 1992.

3.25 Rev. William H. McCormick

In 1889, William H. McCormick and Ben Forbess opened a hardware store in Berthoud. Forbess came to Berthoud from the Hygiene area west of Longmont. McCormick, an Ohio native, had come to the Colorado Territory in 1870, and for two years followed a calling to the United Brethren ministry. McCormick was assigned to a "mission" that encompassed the Cache la Poudre, Big Thompson, Little Thompson, St. Vrain and Left Hand valleys. He traversed the area on horseback.

McCormick married Anna Brunner in 1879. Later she was baptized in the Little Thompson River where it meandered through the Stephen Osborn farm east of Old Berthoud. By the time McCormick staked a claim on a 160-acre homestead north of the town in 1881, a chronic catarrhal condition had forced him to withdraw from the ministry. In 1884, McCormick was elected as Larimer County's representative to the Colorado General Assembly.

Throughout his life, McCormick remained a leader in Berthoud's United Brethren congregation. Many times he pre-

W.H. McCormick (center) at his Berthoud general store. (Berthoud Historical Society)

sided over the funerals of pioneers whom he knew from the valley's early days. In 1900, McCormick fulfilled a life-long dream by making a four-month pilgrimage to the Holy Land. In 1922, he made a large donation to the United Brethren Church, which was used to build a dormitory named McCormick Hall at Bonebrake Seminary in Dayton, Ohio.

From 1889 to 1935, McCormick's Berthoud business prospered. When Forbess withdrew from the partnership in 1892, McCormick converted the operation from a hardware business to a general store. By 1897, his store was stocked with a full line of merchandise. Advertisements published in the Berthoud newspaper proudly proclaimed, "McCormick Sells Everything." A large sign on the roof of his store also heralded that message.

McCormick and his son, Edward, also opened a branch of the business in Highlandlake. The store was moved to the new town of Mead in 1906. That year the McCormicks also established a store in Johnstown.

Rev. William H. McCormick died in February 1932 at the age of 88 years. In 1933, Ed McCormick transformed his father's business into Berthoud's first "help yourself" store. He sold the business to Vern Cady in 1935.

Frances Nielson, Helen Fickel, *The Heritage of Berthoud and the Little Thompson Valley*, Helen McCarty Fickel, Berthoud, Colorado, 1992.

Fort Collins Courier, Jan. 15, 1885; Jan. 30, 1890.

3.26 The End of the 1880s

When the 1880s came to an end, Berthoud had everything in place to assure it would become an important agricultural center of southern Larimer County.

The town was located in what the *Fort Collins Courier* identified as "the best wheat belt in the state." Berthoud also boasted a large flour mill that produced a fine grade of flour that was shipped to markets in Denver, Leadville, Aspen, Glenwood Springs and Santa Fe. The flour was in such demand that in August 1889, when the mill's supply of local wheat was exhausted, 10,000 bushels were shipped in from Kansas. Orders were running 19 carloads behind so the mill operated around the clock to produce 300 sacks of wheat every 24 hours.

In 1887, the depot was equipped with living quarters for the station agent. By this time, the Colorado Central had come under the control of the Union Pacific. The Union Pacific was

Intersection of 3rd Street and Massachusetts Avenue, Berthoud, Colorado, c.1888. (Berthoud Historical Society)

forced into receivership by its bondholders in 1893 and operated as such until 1899. Portions of the Union Pacific were
re-organized as the Colorado & Southern, including the line
through Berthoud to Fort Collins.

The Colorado & Southern was cut off from a direct route
to Cheyenne. Over the course of several years, a new rail line
was constructed in stages from Fort Collins to Wellington, then
north to Dixon. The line was extended to Cheyenne in 1910.

In the fall of 1888, the Town of Berthoud paid $12,000
to the Berthoud Ditch & Reservoir Co. to purchase the gravi-
ty-flow water system that had been built by private subscription in 1887. After the acquisition of the water works, the town
board's attention turned to the placement of water troughs for
horses and the sale of water bonds.

By the close of the 1880s, Berthoud, with its 250 residents,
was considered to be one of Colorado's up-and-coming towns.
In its Berthoud news items of June 20, 1889, the *Loveland
Reporter* noted: "Two seems to be a lucky number here. We
have two groceries, two dry goods stores, two hardwares, two
drugstores, two doctors, two livery and feed stables, two elevators, two wagon makers, two hotels, two church denominations, two dressmakers, and two young ladies who are anxious
to get married."

In addition, the town had a brick schoolhouse, barber
shop, lumberyard, flour mill and what the *Fort Collins Courier*
termed as "greater inducements to settlers than any other town
in northern Colorado."

In June 1889, the Fort Collins newspaper noted, "It is a little remarkable the number of leading citizens of Denver who
are interested in real estate in Berthoud and its adjacent territory...J.C. Hummell owns as fine a section of farming land as
the sun shines upon. Senator H.M. Teller has 320 acres in the
outskirts of the city. A.H. DeFrance of Golden, H.C. Aldritch, a
Denver capitalist, and others are interested in ranch property

in these parts, and most of these are large stockholders in the Farmers' Mill and Elevator Company."

Even though considerable building had taken place in Berthoud in 1889, there was not one house to rent. The town was also much in need of a public hall and a bank.

Fort Collins Courier, Jan. 31, 1889; June 13, 1889; Aug. 15, 1889.

Loveland Reporter, June 20, 1889.

Tiv Wilkins, *Colorado Railroads*, Pruett Publishing Company, Boulder, Colorado, 1974.

3.27 The Big Wind of January 1890

On January 25, 1890, a ferocious windstorm wreaked havoc on northern Colorado. At Berthoud, strong gales toppled the smokestack at the Farmers' mill and caused an additional $200 in damage. Chimneys were blown from roof tops and outbuildings were tossed about like toys. The schoolhouse was damaged and closed for a week for repairs. Northwest of Berthoud a large barn at the Jackson & Lawrence ranch was completely destroyed.

Two miles south of town a freight train pile-up scattered boxcars like match sticks and caused the deaths of two men. In the days following the accident the *Fort Collins Courier* reported: "The accident which occurred on the Union Pacific railroad about 4 o'clock Saturday afternoon near Berthoud, Colo., was much worse than was reported and resulted in the death of Engineer French and Fireman Richmond, who were on the engine of the ill-fated train. The accident was the result of a terrific wind storm. Freight train No. 325 left Denver Saturday morning. John French was the engineer and John Richmond was the fireman. The train consisted of eight cars and a caboose, and was running about fifteen miles an hour as it approached Berthoud. The wind was blowing a furious gale and the air was filled with dust. As the engine rounded a curve and entered a slight cut which was almost filled with sand, the engine seemed to mount the pile of dirt and the next moment plunged in the embankment and turned over, followed by five empty freight cars." Note: The railroad went under its original name, The Colorado Central, but was owned and operated by the Union Pacific.

The engineer, John French, was crushed beneath the tender. John Richmond, the fireman, was scalded by the boiler. Both men died within minutes of the accident.

Many years later, Berthoud historian Ernest Newell recounted a tall tale that circulated through the community following the big wind. It seems that John Barnhardt, who farmed northeast of Berthoud, had picked his corn and stored it in a crib. He then hired Dan Osborn who operated a corn sheller to come to his farm and remove the corn shells from the cobs. After the big wind, Barnhardt sent word to Osborn that there was no need for him to come. Barnhardt claimed that the big wind had blown the cobs through the cracks in the crib and left piles of shelled corn behind!

Fort Collins Courier, Jan. 30, 1890.

Berthoud Bulletin, Apr. 24, 1952.

3.28 Fairbairn Hall

After the Welch Addition was opened to development in 1885, J.W. Dolloff purchased lots on the south side of Mountain Avenue and established the town's first lumberyard. The yard was located east of the Colorado Central tracks.

In November 1886, Dolloff sold his business to John A. Witter of Denver. Witter traded Dolloff 86 mares as part of the transaction. In 1887, the business was purchased by Fairbairn & Hankins. That firm was succeeded by the Fairbairn-Davis Lumber & Coal Company in 1888.

FAIRBAIRN & DAVIS.

———:—HEADQUARTERS FOR:—————

LUMBER, LATH, SHINGLES, PAPER, CEMENT
LIME, HAIR, DOORS & WINDOWS & ALL

—KINDS OF—

BUILDING MATERIAL

ALSO

The best varieties of COAL, both hard & soft

AT PRICES

That Cannot Be Beat.

Berthoud, - Colorado.

Advertisement in *Berthoud Blade*, 1892.

Andrew Fairbairn, a native of Ontario, Canada, came to Larimer County in 1881, settling on a farm near Lone Tree Lake. After Berthoud moved to its new site in the winter of 1883-84, Fairbairn relocated his family to the new town and became a businessman. Irving Davis, who had opened a hardware store in Berthoud in 1886, partnered in the business with Fairbairn.

In 1890, the firm, then known as Fairbairn & Company, erected a new building that allowed operation on a larger scale. In July of that year the *Loveland Reporter* noted, "The new building is 30x34 feet, two stories high. On the ground floor they have an office 10x18 feet furnished to combine comfort and convenience, back and east of the office is a store room where may be found anything that is kept in a first class lumberyard.

"The upper floor is the opera house. This room, 30x34, is reached by a convenient stairway...the hall is seated with 300 chairs...it makes a comfortable hall, with sufficient room to meet the long-felt want of our thriving town."

The newspaper speculated that the new hall would "amply accommodate all town meetings and opera companies that may apply." The tabloid also announced that the second annual meeting of the Berthoud Farmers' Milling & Elevator Company would be held at "Fairbairn's Hall" on July 28, 1890.

Over the years the second-floor room at Berthoud's lumberyard was known as Fairbairn's Hall, Tilton's Hall, Mintener Hall and the "Opera House." Photo c. 1900. (Berthoud Historical Society)

In early August, Berthoud celebrated the opening of the new hall with a "gala-day" that featured horse racing, a baseball game between Berthoud and Longmont, and an evening ball.

The lumberyard building was doubled in size in 1895. The large upstairs room in the building then became known as Tilton's Hall, a name derived from Charles Tilton who managed the lumberyard before trading his farm northeast of Berthoud for it.

In January 1897, the local newspaper appealed to the Berthoud town board to repeal a prohibition on traveling troupes so that Tilton's Hall could become a place of entertainment. That accomplished, patent medicine and minstrel shows were held there beginning in 1896.

In 1899, Andrew Fairbairn regained the lumberyard and added Harvey J. Parish as a partner. In 1908, the lumberyard was sold to the Peter Mintener Lumber Company of Minneapolis and the opera house became known as Mintener Hall.

Over the years the hall played host to public meetings, high school class plays and graduations, basketball games, political caucuses, dances, and the firemen's annual New Year's Eve Ball.

In 1926 the Peter Mintener Company installed a freight elevator in order to convert the old opera house into a storeroom.

Loveland Reporter, Nov. 25, 1886; July 17, 1890; July 31, 1890.

Berthoud Bulletin, Jan. 28, 1897; Jan. 27, 1900.

Loveland Leader, Sept. 9, 1892; Oct. 21, 1892; Dec. 9, 1892.

3.29 Forbess Bros. Shop Destroyed by Fire

The most destructive fire Berthoud had ever experienced
occurred on December 10, 1890, when the Forbess Bros.
blacksmith shop and warehouse on what is now east Mountain
Avenue went up in flames.

One year earlier Ben Forbess of Hygiene and Berthoud's
W.H. McCormick had opened a hardware store in Berthoud
under the name of McCormick & Forbess. In 1889, Forbess also
built a house at 448 Welch Avenue.

In January 1890, Forbess parted from McCormick and took
temporary employment as a traveling agent for the Harrison
Machine Works of Belleville, Illinois. In the spring of 1890
Forbess and his brother formed the firm of Forbess Bros. and
purchased Bill Richardson's blacksmith shop on the south side
of the 200 block of Mountain Avenue. At that location the men
ran a blacksmithing and general repair business as well as the
northern Colorado sales agency for Jumbo steam engines and
Belleville grain separators.

On the night of December 10, 1890, two men who were
boarding in rooms on the second floor of the Forbess Bros.
building were awakened when flames from a blaze in the carpenter and blacksmith shops below burst through the floor. The
boarders escaped in their night clothes and alerted the hose

company. By the time the firemen arrived, all they could save was the adjoining building.

The destruction of their uninsured building resulted in a $2,000 loss for the Forbess brothers. Carpenters Warren Mills and Ben Dix and a house painter named Derby who based their businesses in the building saw their tools destroyed in the great conflagration. Local residents clubbed together to raise $75 for the three tradesmen but the Forbess brothers could not withstand the loss and did not re-establish their business.

Fort Collins Courier, Mar. 28, 1889; Jan. 30, 1890; Apr. 17, 1890; May 1, 1890; Dec. 18, 1890.

Berthoud Bulletin, Mar. 20, 1952.

3.30 Turner House — 1890

Even though two boarding houses operated in Berthoud in 1890, the town considered itself in need of a first class hotel. In February 1890, the *Fort Collins Courier* encouraged Berthoud to brighten its future by building a hotel that might serve as a base for numerous sales agents who circulated throughout northern Colorado. During that era, it was common for hotels to accommodate traveling salesmen by providing a sample room where they could display and sell their wares.

John Shull, operator of one of Berthoud's boarding houses, was considered a likely candidate to build the hotel, but it was ultimately town founder Peter Turner who constructed the Turner House, a hotel at the northeast corner of 4th Street and Massachusetts Avenue in the fall of 1890. A small frame house that had been erected at that site by John Bowman in 1884 was moved to make way for the new building.

The Turner House, a two-story, brick hotel equipped with

dining and sample rooms, was located one block west of the
Colorado Central depot. In the hotel's first year Turner managed the business, but he later leased it to various proprietors
including John Shull. Hotel patrons used the lawn east of
the building as a croquet court until Shull erected the Moon
Theater at that location in 1916.

In December 1890, Berthoud's Presbyterian women hosted
a bazaar and supper at the new hotel to raise money to build
a church. On New Year's Eve 1890, the Berthoud Hose Team
held its second annual masked ball in the dining room of the
Turner House. Music was provided by a small orchestra from
Denver. The previous year the firemen held their ball on the
second floor of the Hubbell & Munson Mercantile building at
the southwest corner of 3rd Street and Massachusetts Avenue.

With the addition
of the Turner House
in 1890, Berthoud
was poised to become
the business center of

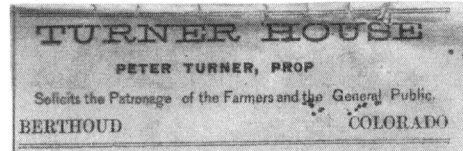

Turner House advertisement in the *Berthoud Blade* (April 22, 1892) and Turner Hotel,
c. 1915. (Berthoud Historical Society)

southern Larimer County. After it opened, the hotel attracted a steady stream of traveling salesmen who worked "the horn" from Denver to Fort Collins to Greeley and made Berthoud one of their bases of operation. Many of them rented rigs at local livery stables in order to travel to Highlandlake, and later, Mead and Johnstown.

Since there was generally a shortage of houses for rent in Berthoud, a number of bachelor businessmen boarded at the Turner House and took their meals in the dining room.

In later years the hotel operated under the names of the Turner Hotel and the Grandview Hotel.

In 1890, the *Fort Collins Courier* encouraged Berthoud to secure a bank in order to keep money generated by the grain elevators and flour mill in the community. Berthoud's second bank opened in 1892 when the Bank of Berthoud was established by New York transplant Thomas Chalmers Bunyan.

Fort Collins Courier, Jan. 31, 1889; Aug. 15, 1889; Feb. 20, 1890; Dec. 25, 1890.

Berthoud Bulletin, Mar. 7, 1952.

Frances Nielson, Helen Fickel, *The Heritage of Berthoud and the Little Thompson Valley*, Helen McCarty Fickel, Berthoud, Colorado, 1992.

Belva Turner Bashor, *Early Berthoud: A History of the Town 1877-1900*, The Old Army Press, Fort Collins, Colorado, 1976, p. 5.

3.31 Masonic Lodge — 1890

Berthoud's second lodge organization, Berthoud Lodge No. 83, A.F. & A.M. (Ancient Free & Accepted Masons) was chartered on May 10, 1890. The Masons had been preceded by Berthoud Lodge No. 37 International Order of Good Templars (I.O.G.T.). The Templars organized their lodge in 1886 and accepted both men and women into their ranks. The Masons were made up exclusively of men.

Charter members of Berthoud's Masonic lodge included Richard M. Hubbell, Harvey J. Parrish, William Clark, F. Irving Davis, James H. McClung, Harrison K. Hankins, John Minor, James Davis, Wilbur Thornton, John F. Hartford, Horace Ferguson, William Hallett, Robert S. Cox, James Harris and Elijah J. Stockwell. Hubbell served as the first Worshipful Master.

One of Berthoud's leading businessmen, Hubbell was a partner with John Y. Munson in the Hubbell & Munson store at the southwest corner of 3rd Street and Massachusetts Avenue. The Masons held meetings on the second floor of the Hubbell & Munson building from the lodge's founding in 1890 until 1906 when a new lodge hall was built at the southeast corner of 4th Street and Massachusetts Avenue.

Many charter members of the Masons were well-known members of the Little Thompson Valley community: Parrish, Clark and Minor lived in the rural district east of Berthoud. When Parrish platted the town of Johnstown on his farm in 1902, he became founder of that new community located on the new Great Western Railway.

Irving Davis and John Hartford were partners in the Davis-Hartford store at the northwest corner of

Berthoud's Masonic Lodge originally met upstairs in the Hubbell & Munson building at 565 3rd Street. Photo c. 1949. (Berthoud Historical Society)

3rd Street and Massachusetts Avenue. McClung farmed south of Berthoud and operated a meat market in a building next door to Hubbell's mercantile. Hankins farmed north of Berthoud.

James Davis was the manager of the Fairbairn-Davis Lumber & Coal Co. Stockwell was a farmer in the Lakeview district north of Berthoud. Ferguson (Hubbell's father-in-law) and Hallett were partners in a ranching operation in the Red Rock district west of Berthoud.

Frances Nielson, Helen Fickel, *The Heritage of Berthoud and the Little Thompson Valley*, Helen McCarty Fickel, Berthoud, Colorado, 1992.

3.32 Hubbell and Munson

Richard "Dick" Hubbell, the first Worshipful Master of Berthoud's Masons, came to Berthoud in 1888. With John Munson as his partner, Hubbell operated a mercantile store across the intersection from the Colorado Central depot. Munson had been a businessman in Berthoud before the town was moved from the river bottom to the bluff.

For a time, the firm of Hubbell & Munson operated in a building owned by Munson. In 1889, they relocated to a new, two-story, brick building at the southwest corner of 3rd Street and Massachusetts Avenue (565 3rd Street). That year Hubbell and Munson also built homes at 444 1st Street and 105 Mountain Avenue respectively.

Dick Hubbell was born in Missouri in 1849. He worked as a printer's devil and owned a newspaper in Richmond, Missouri, before joining the Confederate Army. Following the Civil War, he lost two wives to the white plague [tuberculosis]. In 1874, Hubbell began life anew in Longmont, Colorado, where he joined his brother-in-law in a successful mercantile business.

In Longmont, Hubbell met Miss Anna Ferguson, the daughter of Horace Ferguson. Along with Lord Dunraven, Ferguson was among the first men to claim land in Estes Park. In 1876, Hubbell and Miss Ferguson became the first white couple to be married in the Estes Park Valley. According to Hubbell's memoirs, the minister and guests traveled there in covered wagons and camped overnight.

Richard M. Hubbell
(Berthoud Historical Society)

Hubbell's business partner and fellow Missourian, John Munson, came to Longmont, Colorado, in 1877. He partnered in a mercantile business with Samuel H. Dobbins. In 1882, Munson purchased the Snyder & Grill store that was located in the original Berthoud settlement on the Little Thompson river bottom. Munson moved his building and business to the new town site on the bluff north of the river in the winter of 1883-84.

In the fall of 1884, Munson sold his business to the firm of Mahan & Rowan. Munson went back to Longmont and remained there until 1888 when he returned to Berthoud to partner with Hubbell.

In 1891, Hubbell purchased Munson's interest in the mercantile. Hubbell continued to operate the store until 1895 when he sold to the firm of May & Pollock.

After Munson sold his business interest to Hubbell, he became the first bookkeeper to be employed at the town's new bank. In 1895, Munson left the bank to take a bookkeeping position at the Farmers' Milling & Elevator Co. In 1911, he bought the *Berthoud Bulletin* and operated the newspaper until 1930.

In 1901, Hubbell relocated to Fort Collins where he died in 1917. Munson died in 1932 at the age of 77.

Frances Nielson, Helen Fickel, *The Heritage of Berthoud and the Little Thompson Valley*, Helen McCarty Fickel, Berthoud, Colorado, 1992.

Fort Collins Courier, June 21, 1888; Oct. 17, 1889; Feb. 6, 1890.

Berthoud Blade, 1892

3.33 The *Berthoud Blade*

After the *Berthoud Beacon* ceased publication in November 1886, the community was without a newspaper for nearly five years. During that time public notices were printed elsewhere and posted in the town's stores.

In July 1891, the town's second newspaper came to life when W.T. Michel began publishing the *Berthoud Blade*. The eight-page tabloid was published each Friday. Michel also served as Berthoud's Justice of the Peace and worked as an independent insurance agent.

The *Berthoud Blade* struggled during its first year so Michel used a variety of promotions to increase its readership. In the fall of 1892 for instance, Michel awarded a free one-year subscription to the person who brought the heaviest melon to the *Blade* office.

In April 1893, Grant E. Halderman of Indiana purchased the *Berthoud Blade* and renamed the newspaper the *Berthoud Bulletin*.

During a brief period from January 1897 to March 1898, the town's third newspaper enterprise, the *Berthoud News*, competed with the *Berthoud Bulletin*. The *News* was published by George W. Johnson, who was also the proprietor of the Grandview Hotel.

Berthoud Blade, July 29, 1892; Sept. 16, 1892; Sept. 19, 1892.

Frances Nielson, Helen Fickel, *The Heritage of Berthoud and the Little Thompson Valley*, Helen McCarty Fickel, Berthoud, Colorado, 1992.

3.34 Berthoud's Presbyterians Build a Church

The Presbyterian Church of Berthoud was organized in October 1884, less than a year after the town had been moved up from the river bottom. The first congregation was made up of 22 persons including members of the Bennett, Cole, Hendershott, Keirnes and Newell families. Services were held in a building on present-day 3rd Street where a saloon had been during the town's first few months. Rough plank benches without backs served as seating until 1885 when the congregation's women held a bazaar and supper to raise money to purchase chairs. Later the church met in the town's schoolhouse.

In the winter of 1890-91, Berthoud's Presbyterians built the town's second place of worship when they constructed a brick church on lots donated by railroad man Charles Welch. The lots, valued at $140, sat on the south side of the 500 block of present-day Mountain Avenue. Welch's sole stipulation was that there would be a steeple on the church.

The contract for the church's stone and brick work was let

to Beverly Turner, the son of town founder Peter Turner. He built the walls of the church with bricks produced at a small brickyard located at the north end of Berthoud. The contract for the church's wood-work was given to James Connors. The

Loveland Reporter noted that the church building was to be 40 feet by 36 feet and cost about $1,600.

Since funds were running short when the building approached completion, church elder John Munson suggested building a belfry in place of a vestibule and steeple. The Presbyterians built the belfry but added a steeple when they learned that Welch was serious about his stipulation.

Presbyterian Church, Berthoud, Colorado, c. 1910.
(Berthoud Historical Society)

Frances Nielson, Helen Fickel, *The Heritage of Berthoud and the Little Thompson Valley*, Helen McCarty Fickel, Berthoud, Colorado, 1992.

Loveland Reporter, Nov. 9, 1890.

Helen Fickel, *The History of the First Presbyterian Church, Berthoud, Colorado, 1984.*

3.35 The Berthoud Driving Association

Northern Colorado was wild for various forms of racing in the early 1890s. In 1891 for instance, Loveland's H.G. Shallenberger defeated Berthoud's Amos Mahan in a 100-yard foot race at the volunteer firemen's tournament in Loveland. The following year Mahan faced Loveland's Will Derby in a 100-yard dash that was held on Welch Avenue in Berthoud. The men vied for a $50 prize. The identity of the winner is not known.

On July 4, 1894, Linden Street in Fort Collins was the site of a bicycle race in which firemen from Boulder, Longmont, Berthoud, Loveland, Greeley, Cheyenne, Laramie, and Fort Collins participated. The race was part of a celebration that commemorated the 118th anniversary of the signing of the Declaration of Independence.

The most popular of all racing events of the time began in the early 1890s when towns along Colorado's northern Front Range, including Berthoud, formed driving associations and sponsored harness racing. Meets generally took place over a three-day period and featured trotting, pacing, and running races for purses of $100 or more.

In 1891, a group of Berthoud men that included Andy Fairbairn filed articles of incorporation for the Berthoud Driving Association. The group purchased 16 acres of land at the east edge of town from R.M. Hubbell and John McCormick to be the site of the Berthoud Driving Park. They graded a half-mile track, erected a tall wooden fence and built a grandstand.

From 1891 through 1894, the Berthoud Driving Association held spring and fall meets at the park. The races attracted up to 500 spectators and filled the Turner House to capacity. Towns on the northern Colorado race circuit included Greeley, Fort Collins, Loveland, Berthoud, Longmont, and Boulder.

Berthoud's Ed Sperry owned one of Colorado's premier trotters, a mare named "Lizzie S." Boulder's "Motion Gold Dust" and Longmont's "Bertie M." were her main competitors in the races held in Berthoud in June 1892.

Among the Berthoud men who entered horses in local meets were George W. Keirnes (and his horse, Duke Temple), Cornelius "Con" Clark (Blizzard and Lucky), Jason Taylor (Jay Gould), John McCormick (Red Miller), Henry Longdon (Humpy), E.W. Ellermeyer (Billy), W.O. "Bill" Pulliam (Kitty), and Jim Davis (Billy Miller). Other Berthoud racers were W.B. Forbess, John Martindale, Andy Fairbairn, Charles Blackwell and James Connors.

Towns outside the racing circuit that were represented at the Berthoud races were Denver, Platteville, Fort Lupton and Eaton.

In January 1895, however, the *Berthoud Bulletin* announced a trustee's sale of the Berthoud Driving Association. Debt, not disinterest, had brought an end to harness racing in Berthoud.

Loveland Leader, June 3, 1892; July 29, 1892.

Fort Collins Courier, May 24, 1894.

Berthoud Bulletin, Apr. 24, 1952.

3.36 Ed Sperry

Before Ed Sperry earned a reputation as a harness racer, he served as Berthoud's first town marshal and street supervisor. Sperry was only 23 years of age when he took office in October 1888. He resigned from the position the following February.

Sperry had assumed the responsibilities of manhood at an early age. In 1878, the 13-year-old Sperry came to Central City from Ottumwa, Iowa, with the understanding that he would send for his younger brothers and sister once he was established. In 1883, Sperry and his brother, Stephen, found jobs as farm hands on Major John Kerr's farm west of the original Berthoud settlement.

In January 1890, Sperry married Lulie Blackwell, the daughter of local general store operator Charles R. Blackwell. Mr. and Mrs. Sperry added sons Walter and Charles and daughter, Marhon, to their family in the following years.

In the early 1890s, Sperry built a house at present-day 413 County Rd. 8. The home was located beside the Berthoud Driving Park east of Berthoud. Sperry and his prize trotter, Lizzie S., earned such notoriety in harness racing circles that in 1893, he was able to sell the mare to a Denver man for the considerable sum of $1,250.

In 1896, Sperry moved his family from Berthoud to the bustling mining camp of Eldora. He became town marshal of this mountain boomtown that boasted a total of nine saloons, dance halls and gambling houses.

Ed Sperry and one of his trotters. (Berthoud Historical Society)

In November 1900, Sperry earned the reputation as Boulder County's "most fearless peace officer." In a protest over unpaid wages, an angry mob of miners had stormed the home of the mine operator, riddled it with bullets and set it ablaze. Sperry restored order and extinguished the fire despite threats that he would be shot. Within the year Sperry was rewarded for his heroics by being named Under Sheriff of Boulder County, an office he held for two terms.

Sperry eventually moved to Wyoming but returned to Colorado to file a homestead claim in North Park. By 1932, Sperry was back in Berthoud where with his son, Charles, he opened a pool and billiard hall in a ground-floor room of the Odd Fellows Building at 335 Mountain Avenue.

Ed Sperry witnessed the growth of Berthoud from a handful of buildings on the Little Thompson river bottom in 1883 to a town of more than 1,000 residents at the time of his death. During his 70 years he rubbed shoulders with lawbreakers, gamblers, horsemen, miners and homesteaders. Thrust into manhood in his youth, Ed Sperry was a fearless character who carried the mantle of Berthoud's first lawman.

Ed Sperry passed away in Berthoud in 1935. His obituary in the *Berthoud Bulletin* noted that the town's old timers recalled Sperry as a "good, square man."

Berthoud Bulletin, Sept. 26, 1935.

3.37   The Berthoud Cornet Band

In April 1892, W.T. Michel, editor of the *Berthoud Blade*, organized a brass band that purchased instruments with money donated by community members. Michel played the baritone horn and acted as the president of the 11-member group named the Berthoud Cornet Band. Attorney J. Mack Mills doubled as the band's conductor and one of seven cornet players. The remaining band members included Beverly Turner, Harry Newell, L. Van Delinder, Mark Warfle, Doc Searcy, George Rose, Dan Osborn, Ben Sexton and Charles Blackwell.

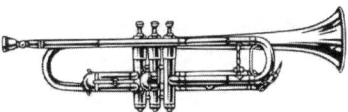

In announcing the formation of the band Michel wrote, "A brass band is to the prosperity and comforts of business people in civil life what it is to the comfort and courage of the soldier in military life. When the business man is weary and tired, and dull monotony seems to reign supreme, then it is the band that steps in and while the harmony of the instruments blends with the silent music of the soul and the heart throbs in unison with the big bass drum, dull monotony is changed into active impulse and he forgets that he was weary and tired and ever anon the music of the band ascends heaven ward and announces to the world that we are pressing onward and upward in the battle of life. Music is the sunshine and the climate of the soul and it floods the heart with a perfect June. The parent who can look into the eyes of his own child, as the band begins to play, and there witness the expressions of joy as they flash forth from his shining countenance, without thanking God for the brass band is unworthy to be styled a parent."

The Berthoud Cornet Band took its civic duties seriously in 1892 when it escorted local school children in a Columbus Day parade down the streets of Berthoud. Afterward the band returned to the school and gave a concert. In the spring of 1894 the cornet band was reorganized as an orchestra.

Berthoud Blade, Apr. 22, 1892.

Loveland Leader, Oct. 21, 1892.

3.38   First School Commencement

The first school commencement to be held in the town of Berthoud took place on May 6, 1892, at the newly constructed Presbyterian Church. The ceremony marked the graduation of four young women from eighth grade at the Berthoud School: Lillie Gertrude Baird, Susan "Susie" Sunshine Turner, Susannah Emaline "Emma" Flora and Blanche E. Wright.

Lillie Baird was the daughter of C.M. Baird, one of the town's masons and plasterers. Berthoud founder Peter Turner was the father of 15-year-old Susie Turner. Emma Flora, who was 19 years old, was the daughter of butcher William Flora. Twenty-two-year-old Blanche Wright was the daughter of retired merchant Charles A. Wright. Turner, Flora and Wright trained to become teachers and were hired at various times to teach at the Berthoud School.

In the fall of 1899 the Berthoud School offered ninth grade classes for the first time. In the following years 10th, 11th, and 12th grade classes were added. In 1903, the Berthoud School hosted its first 12th grade graduation ceremony. The event took place at the opera house.

Frances Nielson, Helen Fickel, *The Heritage of Berthoud and the Little Thompson Valley*, Helen McCarty Fickel, Berthoud, Colorado, 1992.

3.39   Steeple-Building Rivalry

When Charles C. Welch donated land to Berthoud's Presbyterians for the site of a church, he stipulated that the new church have a tall steeple.

In later years Presbyterian Church charter member S. Ernest Newell recalled, "When they built the church they ran short of

money, so Mr. Munson suggested they build a belfry on top of
the church. About that time my mother (Mrs. Carrie Newell)
was coming from Denver on the train, and Mr. Welch was also
on the train. He wanted to know when they were going to build
the steeple on the church. She told him what they had decided,
and Welch replied, 'You tell John Munson that a dog house
on a church might answer for a steeple in Missouri, but not in
Colorado. If you folks expect to get a deed to those lots you had
better build a steeple.' So they proceeded to build a steeple."
(John Munson, the object of Welch's wrath and a church elder,
was a native Missourian.)

The Presbyterians worked quickly and by December 1892
had added a steeple to their church. Local carpenter Warren L.
Mills completed the project. Later the Presbyterians joked that
the cost of the steeple, combined with the cost of the vestibule,
exceeded the amount of money spent to build the church!

When Berthoud's United Brethren congregation got wind of
Welch's ultimatum to the Presbyterians, they rushed to erect
a steeple on the church they had built in 1886 at the corner of

A steeple was added to the United Brethren church (center) in 1893 after the town's
churches were swept up in a steeple-building rivalry. (c. 1903, Berthoud Historical
Society)

4th Street and Turner Avenue. They also hired Mills and when he was finished in January 1893, the steeple rose 67 feet above ground level.

A third church steeple appeared in Berthoud in 1893 when the Christian Church was built at the northeast corner of 4th Street and Welch Avenue. Unlike the United Brethren and Presbyterian churches, a bell tower with a steeple was part of the building's original construction. Warren Mills and his son, J. Mack Mills, built the church.

Berthoud Bulletin, Apr. 24, 1952.

Berthoud Blade, Sept. 2, 1892; Nov. 11, 1892; Feb. 3, 1893.

3.40 The Christian Church

After Berthoud moved from the Little Thompson river bottom in the winter of 1883-84, the local United Brethren congregation continued to use the schoolhouse at Old Berthoud as a church. Use of the school for services ended in 1886 after they constructed a new brick church building in the relocated town.

A group of church-goers, including Walter "Pappy" Fenton, Davis Baxter and Stephen Osborn, also held services at the Old Berthoud school until 1892. That year they moved their place of worship to Fairbairn's Hall, the large upstairs room in the lumberyard building in Berthoud. Their preacher, Elder Harris of the Christian Church, delivered sermons on Saturday nights. Harris also preached at the Sunnyside school northeast of Berthoud.

In the fall of 1892, the small Christian Church congregation purchased a building site at the northeast corner of 4th Street and Welch Avenue. In January 1893, church members

Warren Mills and his son, J. Mack Mills, began building the church. When it was completed the town of Berthoud had three churches serving its 300 citizens.

In January 1915, the Christian Church was nearly destroyed by fire. Efforts to save the frame structure were hampered by a frozen water hydrant. With an insurance settlement of $664.24, the congregation repaired the building and resumed services. The church, however, failed to thrive and closed its doors in 1920.

An effort to revive the congregation in 1925 proved unsuccessful, and following a few years of use by a German Congregational church, the building was torn down in 1929. Materials salvaged from the structure were used to construct a dormitory at the Cotner College summer campus located on Frend Neville's Sylvan Dale Ranch near the mouth of the Big Thompson Canyon west of Loveland.

The Christian Church at the northeast corner of 4th Street and Welch Avenue. (Berthoud Historical Society)

Loveland Leader, Nov. 18, 1892; Dec. 23, 1892.

Frances Nielson, Helen Fickel, *The Heritage of Berthoud and the Little Thompson Valley*, Helen McCarty Fickel, Berthoud, Colorado, 1992.

Berthoud Bulletin, Jan. 7, 1897; Jan. 29, 1915; Feb. 26, 1915; June 7, 1929.

3.41   Foresman & McCarty Drugstore

The arrivals of Harley H. Foresman and David W. McCarty to Berthoud in 1892 provided the fledgling town with two young businessmen who became outstanding citizens. Their business venture, the Foresman & McCarty drugstore, flourished until 1932.

Dr. David W. McCarty
(Berthoud Historical Society)

Foresman and McCarty came to Colorado from Iowa after Foresman's brother-in-law, Fred Welty, advised them that a drugstore could be purchased in the eight-year-old town of Berthoud. Welty farmed near the neighboring community of Highlandlake.

In October 1892, Foresman and McCarty purchased the stock of Dr. L.C. Tilden's drugstore. They remodeled the building, located in

Harley Foresman and family
(Berthoud Historical Society)

the 500 block of 3rd Street, installing a new store front and upgrading the floor. A.C. Atwood was hired to operate the jewelry department. Foresman supervised the sales of a general line of merchandise, dispensed prescriptions and marshaled the operation of a soda fountain. McCarty maintained a medical office in the back of the store and kept a horse and buggy on call at Sim Jefferes's livery stable for house calls.

Foresman and his family made their home at 526 5th Street. McCarty, a 23-year-old bachelor, rented a room at the Turner House and took his meals in the hotel's dining room. McCarty maintained that living arrangement until his marriage to a local girl, Jennie Fagan, in 1906.

Like many businesses in the 500 block of 3rd Street, the Foresman & McCarty drugstore was housed in a long, narrow building. A pair of plate glass windows flanked the front entrance that was shaded by an awning emblazoned with the words "Foresman & McCarty Druggists." In 1892, a wooden boardwalk provided access to the drugstore and neighboring businesses along 3rd Street.

In June 1910, Elmer (left) and Floyd Clymer (right) posed in their automobile in front of the Foresman & McCarty drugstore before unsuccessfully attempting a cross-country automobile trip to Spokane, Washington. (Berthoud Historical Society)

Foresman and McCarty became lifelong residents of the Berthoud community. Both were involved in church and civic affairs, local politics and the operation of farms they owned in the Little Thompson Valley. The Foresman & McCarty drugstore closed shortly after Foresman's death in 1932. McCarty passed away five years later. Both men were buried in Berthoud's Greenlawn Cemetery.

Berthoud Blade, Oct. 7, 1892.

Berthoud Bulletin, Feb. 18, 1897.

Frances Nielson, Helen Fickel, *The Heritage of Berthoud and the Little Thompson Valley*, Helen McCarty Fickel, Berthoud, Colorado, 1992.

3.42 New Arrivals in the 1890s

In a fashion similar to the homesteaders who flocked to the valley in the 1880s, businessmen came to Berthoud in the 1890s as the town began to boom. During both decades, a handful of

Farmer-turned-businessman James H. McClung (in white butcher's apron nearest open door) at the Berthoud Meat Market in 1899. (Berthoud Historical Society)

homesteaders who had profited from land claims moved to town and became businessmen. These men included Rev. William H. McCormick, Andrew Fairbairn, James H. McClung, John R. Preston, John C. Shull, Marvin D. Whipple and Chalmon Wray. The town also attracted numerous tradesmen who helped boost its economy.

The year 1890 brought Alfred G. Bimson to Berthoud from Illinois. Bimson established his first blacksmith shop in a frame building on east Mountain Avenue. He upgraded his operation in 1893 by purchasing two lots from town founder Peter Turner and hiring mason J.C. Lurvey to construct a 20- by 30-foot stone building. Bimson remained in business at his "Stone Shop" for nearly 50 years.

Bimson was among Berthoud's best blacksmiths. During the early years when Berthoud's economy was based on agriculture, Bimson shoed horses, sharpened plows, repaired wagons and forged tools. In the 1920s, he shifted to the production of decorative ironwork such as benches, gates and fireplace andirons. As his career drew to a close during World War II, Bimson transformed discarded iron files and car springs into nearly 400 "jungle knives"

Blacksmith A.G. Bimson (left) hired stonemason J.C. Lurvey to build his "Stone Shop" in 1893. The Little Thompson Valley Pioneer Museum currently occupies the building at 228 Mountain Avenue in Berthoud. (Berthoud Historical Society)

that were supplied to American soldiers based in the Pacific Theatre.

During his life, Bimson added his fine tenor voice to the United Brethren church choir. He dabbled in photography and served as a town trustee (1893-95) and mayor (1897-1900). A firm prohibitionist whose wife Margaret was a member of the local Women's Christian Temperance Union, Bimson worked to keep saloons out of Berthoud during his tenure as mayor. In 1904, he made an unsuccessful bid for Larimer County Sheriff on the Prohibition Party ticket. Bimson Avenue and the Bimson Addition to the town of Berthoud (1904) took their names from the pioneer businessman who passed in 1947.

Arthur F. Brown also came to Berthoud in 1890. Formerly a salesman for the Deering Company, Brown sold farm implements at the Davis-Hartford Mercantile and oversaw the company's undertaking business. Since Davis & Hartford promised their customers "...everything from the cradle to the grave," Brown sold caskets, scheduled the company's horse-drawn hearse and supplied chairs for home funerals.

In June 1893, Brown purchased four lots at the northeast corner of 5th Street and Massachusetts Avenue from Peter Turner for $800 where he built a "commodious dwelling." Brown served as Berthoud's mayor (1892-93) and postmaster (1902-08) and also as a Larimer County Commissioner (1894-97).

In 1892, Thomas Chalmers Bunyan came to Berthoud from Ballston Spa, New York, to open the Bank of Berthoud. Formerly a school superintendent, Bunyan established his new bank in the building erected for that purpose at the corner of 3rd Street and Mountain Avenue in 1886. With Bunyan came an infusion of New York capital that backed local enterprises such as the Berthoud Driving Association, and helped solidify the village's status as the business center of southern Larimer County. Bunyan's descendants continued to operate the bank for more than a century.

In 1895, Richard M. Hubbell sold his mercantile store at the corner of 3rd Street and Massachusetts Avenue to Canadian brothers-in-law Duncan M. May and Charles G. Pollock. The firm of May & Pollock, which boasted Berthoud's largest dry goods store, remained in operation until 1928.

Thomas Chalmers Bunyan
(Berthoud Historical Society)

D.M. May, the older of the brothers-in-law, came to Colorado in hopes of improving his health. He served as Berthoud Town Clerk in 1900 and as mayor from 1900 to 1903. May and his wife Mary lived in a house at the southwest corner of 4th Street and Mountain Avenue (no longer standing) that was built in 1888 by John and Minnie Hartford.

Charles Pollock (center) at the May & Pollock store, c. 1905.
(Berthoud Historical Society)

Charles Pollock, the younger brother-in-law by 13 years, was wed to Nettie Davis, the daughter of Irving Davis who owned the general store (no longer standing) across the street from the May & Pollock store (565 3rd Street). The Pollocks lived in the house at 739 Mountain Avenue.

May and Pollock made Berthoud their homes for the remainder of their days, passing on in 1913 and 1962 respectively.

Berthoud Bulletin, Mar. 3, 1893.

Fort Collins Courier, June 8, 1893.

Frances Nielson, Helen Fickel, *The Heritage of Berthoud and the Little Thompson Valley*, Helen McCarty Fickel, Berthoud, Colorado, 1992.

3.43 Hard Times in 1893

Colorado's economy was sent reeling in 1893 when the price of silver crashed. Up to that time much of the state's prosperity resulted from the production of this precious metal. When silver markets plummeted, prices fell from 83 to 62 cents per ounce, and the Panic of 1893 was on.

By the summer of 1893, several Denver banks had closed their doors and numerous businesses around the state—including mines and smelters—had ceased operation. Colorado's prosperity ended, followed by hard times and high unemployment.

Men without jobs hopped trains and searched across the country for work. That the 1893 Panic was felt in Berthoud was evidenced by Mayor Alfred Bimson's request that citizens refrain from feeding the tramps overrunning the town. That stance was softened in April 1897 when the Town of Berthoud began purchasing meals for "vagrants, bums, paupers and tramps" at the cost of 20 cents each.

Rural communities like Berthoud were hit especially hard by a decline in the price of wheat. The crisis deepened when farmers increased their grain acreage and flooded the market with surplus wheat. After the Panic, local farmers, who had sold their wheat for $1 per bushel in 1884, considered themselves fortunate to receive 27 cents per bushel.

Wilbur Thornton (*History of Larimer County, Colorado*)

The low market price for wheat was aggravated by the discovery in August 1893 that the Farmers' Milling & Elevator Company's manager, Frank Crane, had made a practice of speculating with the company's funds. The company's board of directors forced Crane to resign, charged him with embezzlement and had him arrested. Wilbur Thornton was hired to fill Crane's position. Thornton quickly implemented an across-the-board reduction of employee wages and eliminated several positions to reduce the mill's operating cost by about two-thirds.

Following Crane's arrest the *Loveland Leader* opined: "The arrest last week of Mr. Crane upon a trumped up charge growing out of the badly mixed affairs of the Berthoud roller mills, has been the event of interest in Berthoud this week. The fact that the division of sentiment in the matter is similar to that in the late election over the question of [liquor] license or no license, in which Mr. Crane took an active part, the exceptions being in favor of Mr. Crane, make it look very much as though spite is at the bottom of it all...To charge such an influential citizen with a crime so niggardly, under such circumstances, is a serious matter, and we sincerely hope that the courts will be able to mete out justice to both the innocent and the guilty, and that without delay."

Crane, a Berthoud town trustee who had made enemies for favoring the issuance of liquor licenses, was later absolved of any wrongdoing.

The BERTHOUD ROLLER MILLS,

Grain and Chop Feed always on hand.
Dealers in Barley and Potatoes. Alfalfa and Clover Seed Bought and Sold.

Patronize Home Industry.

After his departure, Crane and two employees who had also been fired in Berthoud leased the Grange flour mill east of Longmont. Crane later went into business in Denver.

The plant of the Berthoud Farmers' Milling & Elevator Company was also known as the Berthoud Roller Mills. (*Berthoud Bulletin*, Oct. 5, 1894)

Berthoud Bulletin, May 8, 1852.

Belva Turner Bashor, *Early Berthoud: A History of the Town 1877-1900*, The Old Army Press, Fort Collins, Colorado, 1976, p. 65.

Fort Collins Courier, Aug. 3, 1893.

Leroy Hafen and Ann Hafen, *The Colorado Story*, The Old West Publishing Company, Denver, Colorado, 1953, p. 264.

Loveland Leader, Aug. 11, 1893.

3.44 Streets Get New Names

Berthoud's streets were numbered and re-named in May 1893. Mayor Arthur F. Brown and town trustees William H. McCormick, Alfred Bimson, Daniel Mahan and Frank Crane were responsible for changing the names on Peter Turner's original 1883 plat. The reasons for the changes were not recorded.

The new system called for the town's north-south thorough-fares to be identified as numbered streets. All east-west thoroughfares were distinguished as avenues with names. Pine St., the only north-south road that existed on Turner's 1883 plat, gained a new identity as 4th Street. The names of the three east-west thoroughfares that Turner originally identified as Thompson, Welch and Munson streets were given the names of Mountain, Massachusetts and Turner avenues respectively.

Mountain Avenue, originally named Thompson Street by Turner, may have taken its name from the view of Longs Peak and Mount Meeker seen in the Front Range skyline due west of Berthoud.

Massachusetts Avenue, initially named for businessman John Y. Munson, may have been an understated tribute to F. Irving Davis, Berthoud's first mayor and a native of that state, whose personal residence and business were located on the street.

The town's founder, Peter Turner, was the namesake of Turner Avenue. The east-west street located one block south of Mountain Avenue, a byway that did not exist on Turner's plat, was given the name Welch Avenue. It ran through the Welch Addition that Charles C. Welch added to the southern border of Berthoud in 1885.

A second east-west street that extended toward a shallow lake at the northwest edge of town, was given the name Lake Street.

In other business at the May meeting, Berthoud's town trustees voted to reduce the town marshal position to half-time status and pay 25 cents an hour. As a result, acting marshal William C. Fenton resigned. Just two months later Fenton's successor, Joseph Dewey, dealt with Berthoud's first murder. Dewey had worked in the rock quarries near Lyons before coming to Berthoud.

Belva Turner Bashor, *Early Berthoud: A History of the Town 1877-1900*, The Old Army Press, Fort Collins, Colorado, 1976, p. 63.

3.45 Cresswell Shooting

The first murder within Berthoud's town limits was committed on June 26, 1893. That evening while working behind the counter at his confectionery shop, shopkeeper David F. Cresswell shot an inebriated railroad section hand named Pat Buckley. Buckley had insulted Cresswell after being refused another drink.

Joseph Dewey, Berthoud's town marshal, happened to be in Cresswell's confectionery shop at the time and was caught off guard when Cresswell grabbed a 38-caliber revolver and shot Buckley twice in the chest. Dr. David McCarty rushed to the scene to examine the wounded man and had him removed to the Turner House. Buckley died a few days later after much suffering.

A lanky and well-liked man who had been known as "Long Pat," Buckley was remembered by his friends as a good natured Irishman who, "...when in liquor was apt to give offense by the freedom of his actions."

Even though there was no question that Cresswell had shot Buckley, two trials were required to determine his punishment. At the first trial held in September 1893, the law firm of Bailey & Garbutt from Fort Collins presented a convincing defense that Creswell's irrational act had resulted from a sunstroke that altered his temperament several years earlier. After 43 hours of deliberation and a jury divided between verdicts of second degree murder or voluntary manslaughter, the trial ended in a hung jury.

At Cresswell's second trial in March 1894, the jury deliberated at length before convicting him of voluntary manslaughter. He was sentenced to five and one-half years in the Colorado State Penitentiary. By that time, Cresswell had spent nearly a year in the Larimer County Jail.

On December 26, 1895, the *Herald Democrat* of Leadville

reported that on Christmas Day a warden's pardon had been extended to David F. Creswell who was subsequently released from the Colorado State Penitentiary in Canon City. The tabloid explained, "Every Christmas day, at the exercises in the chapel, the warden grants a pardon to some prisoner whose conduct while in that institution has been a model and whose reformation is such as to make him not a dangerous man. The pardon is made by the governor on the recommendation of the warden."

David Cresswell died in Pueblo in 1927.

Loveland Leader, June 30, 1893.

Fort Collin Courier, Sept. 28, 1893; Oct. 5, 1893; Mar. 29, 1894.

Herald Democrat, Dec. 26, 1895.

3.46 "Rusticating"

Fishing was a popular pastime for the valley's early residents. Irrigation reservoirs filled with water from the Big Thompson River were among their favorite fishing holes. Farmers considered fish in these reservoirs to be their property and charged for fishing. There were disputes when several farms bordered a lake and landowners argued over who had the right to collect fees.

Berthoud men rusticating in the mountains. (Left to right) John Stryker, Gene Smith, two unidentified men from the Saltzman family, S.F. Curtis, Bert Curtis. (Berthoud Historical Society)

One such dispute played out in the *Berthoud Bulletin* in the summer of 1893 when W.T.W. "Alphabet" Smith informed the newspaper that 25 pounds of catfish, sunfish and perch had been seined and stolen from his lake northeast of Berthoud. In the next issue of the newspaper Smith's neighbor, A.A. Knott, replied that the 3,000 catfish he had stocked in the lake belonged to him. Knott added that the lake was filled with 40 shares of his water, 27 shares that belonged to his brother-in-law Jake Welty, and a mere seven shares owned by Smith. Knott claimed that Smith had no right to sell the fish in "his" lake for three cents per pound.

The following week, Smith offered up numbers to show that the largest percentage of the lake's area was on his property. He also disputed Knott's calculation of Home Supply and Handy

Duck hunting party of Berthoud boys including Claude Fairbairn (upper left), William Shreves (upper right), G.A. "Duck" Turner (lower left) and Sid Davis (lower right), c. 1900. (Berthoud Historical Society)

Ditch shares in the lake. Nothing further appeared in the newspaper.

In the 1890s, it was common for local men to "go rusticating" in the mountains. They loaded their wagons with hunting and fishing gear, left their wives at home, and rumbled up the Cache la Poudre or Big Thompson canyons to camp. At that time, there wasn't a road in the Big Thompson Canyon so travelers used a road located on the high ground south of the river.

Mark Smith
(Berthoud Historical Society)

In July 1893, a group of Berthoud men including Mark Smith (Alphabet Smith's father), Bill Turner, Josh Barr, Bill Harris, George Buzzard, Frank Mount, and a fellow named Patterson, went rusticating in the Big Thompson Canyon. The trip ended in tragedy.

Smith, a 77-year-old resident of the Sunnyside district northeast of Berthoud, sustained what appeared to be a minor injury when the men's wagon overturned and sent them sprawling to the ground. A cut over Smith's right eye was bandaged before the men made camp for the night.

The next morning the men continued up the road to Estes Park. Smith got out of the wagon and started walking down Dixon Hill after telling the others that he would fish up the river and meet them at camp. Some three hours later, another party of travelers discovered Smith lying unconscious by the roadside. His eye was badly swollen and covered with blood. The injured man was loaded into a wagon and rushed to Loveland where he died from a hemorrhage.

Berthoud Blade, Aug. 26, 1893; Sept. 2, 1893; Sept. 29, 1893.

Loveland Ledger, July 7, 1893.

3.47 Stone Walks, Electric Lights and Telephone Service

In 1893, Berthoud turned its attention to sidewalks, electric lights and telephones. That year sandstone sidewalks extending into residential neighborhoods began replacing wooden boardwalks in the town's tiny business district. One stone sidewalk stretched for nearly five blocks along the south side of Mountain Avenue from 1st Street to the Presbyterian Church. The Union Pacific Railroad also installed stone crosswalks at their tracks and switches.

The following year, several stone crosswalks were laid across muddy street intersections. Sidewalks in residential neighborhoods that had been installed before street and lot lines were established were lined with new walks.

In 1893, the Berthoud Town Board determined a location for a dynamo that would power electric lights. Just two years later, the Town purchased and installed five oil-burning street lamps.

 Telephone service came to Berthoud in October 1893 when the Colorado Telephone Company constructed a toll line connecting Greeley and Fort Collins with Denver. Berthoud's first telephone was placed in the Davis-Hartford Mercantile at the corner of 3rd Street and Massachusetts Avenue. The toll to make a five-minute call from Berthoud to Fort Collins was 25 cents. This was considered more reasonable than sending a telegraph. A second telephone was installed in the manager's office at the Fairbairn & Davis lumberyard.

Local residents learned about the dangers of "telephonic communication" in September 1894 when the *Berthoud Bulletin* reported, "Lightning entered the telephone in the Davis-Hartford store during Friday's thunderstorm and shook up things pretty lively for a few seconds. Arthur Brown had his ear to the phone at the time and received a shock that nearly knocked him down. Aside from this scare but little damage was done."

In 1901, the Colorado Telephone Company published a "List of Subscribers" in Fort Collins, Loveland, Berthoud and Livermore." Most of the 38 Berthoud entrees were linked to business offices or "ranches" in the countryside but town dwellers J.B. Clymer, H.P. Dennis, A.A. Knott, H.A. Lovejoy, J.Y. Munson and J.H. Newell had telephones in their homes.

Wooden boardwalks in front of the business buildings along 3rd Street in Berthoud in 1890. (Berthoud Historical Society)

Loveland Leader, Dec. 23, 1892; Aug. 18, 1893.

Fort Collins Courier, Oct. 19, 1893; Nov. 16, 1893; Apr. 19, 1894; Dec. 27, 1894.

Berthoud Bulletin, Sept. 14, 1894; Apr. 21, 1906.

Frances Nielson, Helen Fickel, *The Heritage of Berthoud and the Little Thompson Valley*, Helen McCarty Fickel, Berthoud, Colorado, 1992.

3.48 Farmers Diversify

In the early 1890s, due in part to the crash of wheat prices in 1893, Little Thompson Valley farmers explored sources of income from other crops. They broadened their operations by fattening hogs and sheep, planting fruit orchards, selling dairy products and growing potatoes and alfalfa.

The dependence of local farmers on wheat led *Berthoud Bulletin* editor Grant Haldeman to call for change in January 1894 when he proclaimed, "More potatoes, less wheat should be the motto of northern Colorado farmers henceforth." A month later Haldeman announced that George and Jake Welty had fattened 35 hogs on equal parts of corn, barley and wheat and hauled in a "snug sum." Haldeman asked other farmers to report on their hog feeding and noted, "It may be the means of inducing others to embark in stock raising, rather than 'wheating,' often an unprofitable occupation."

Potato harvest near Berthoud photographed by A.G. Bimson, c. 1895. (Berthoud Historical Society)

Berthoud Produce Company warehouse at the intersection of 3rd Street and Massachusetts Avenue in Berthoud, c. 1914. (Berthoud Historical Society)

The *Bulletin* also announced that Berthoud needed a potato warehouse and predicted that any enterprising individual who backed the project would profit. The tabloid added, with dead certainty, that potatoes would become one of the chief crops of local farmers.

A short time later, banker Thomas C. Bunyan, merchant F. Irving Davis, and James Gregg organized the Berthoud Produce Company. They built a 30- by 60-foot warehouse near the depot at the northeast corner of 3rd Street and Massachusetts Avenue. The two-story, pressed brick building with full basement was declared complete in October 1894 after being outfitted with equipment needed "...for the rapid handling of potatoes and all farm produce."

Ironically the warehouse was razed in 1919 to make way for a grain elevator.

Potato harvesting crew at work near Berthoud photographed by A.G. Bimson, c. 1895. (Berthoud Historical Society)

William H. McCormick, who had expanded his hardware business into a general store, added a selection of seed potatoes that included Early Rose, Early Ohio and Snow Flake varieties. In October 1894, the *Bulletin* announced that the person who brought the largest potato to its office by November 15 would win a one-year's subscription to the newspaper.

A month later when the pace of the potato harvest lagged, the newspaper cautioned, "Some of the farmers are getting uneasy about their potato crops. The southward flight of ducks and geese betokens the coming winter while the festive spud diggers are mining tubers with the greatest leisure."

In the early 1890s, local farmers also planted large plots of raspberries and orchards filled with cherry, apple, peach and plum trees. Mark H. Warfle, an original employee of Berthoud's flour mill, purchased 15 acres at the north end of Berthoud where he established a fruit farm with 600 cherry trees. Warfle's "Berthoud Fruit Farm" was located northwest of the intersection of present-day 4th Street and Bunyan Avenue.

Warfle operated a chicken hatchery at that location while his trees grew to maturity. Later he earned a handsome profit by shipping fruits and vegetables to mining towns like Leadville where fresh produce was in high demand.

In 1894, the *Bulletin* issued a call for a creamery to be built in Berthoud. Up to that time, local dairymen had hauled their milk and cream to market in Longmont. Later that year a creamery was established in a frame building that sat east of Alfred Bimson's blacksmith shop on East Mountain Avenue.

Prices paid for potatoes fell short of expectations in 1894. Farmers already growing alfalfa turned more attention to that crop since it was gaining popularity as feed for fattening lambs. Profits earned by "feeding sheep" soon captured the interest of all farmers in northern Colorado.

Workers covering raspberry canes with soil to protect them from the winter's cold. (c. 1895, Berthoud Historical Society)

Berthoud Bulletin, Aug. 3, 1894; Sept. 7, 1894; Sept. 21, 1894; Oct. 19, 1894; July 16, 1904; Sept. 14, 1904.

Berthoud Blade, Nov. 11, 1892.

Fort Collins Courier, Dec. 13, 1894.

3.49 Sheep Feeding

The rise of the sheep feeding industry got underway in 1889 when a fall blizzard stranded a shipment of 2,400 lambs at Walsenburg in southern Colorado. By the time the railroad tracks were cleared, the lambs had grown so scraggly that they were shipped to Fort Collins to be fattened, rather than sending them directly to markets in the East. At Fort Collins, where

Albert A. Knott
(*Berthoud Bulletin*, Sept. 7, 1901)

alfalfa hay was cheap and plentiful, the lambs were fattened and sold for a profit. The industry grew quickly and soon nearly a million lambs were being fed in Northern Colorado.

Sheep feeding gained a foothold in the Berthoud area in 1890 when two farmers and brothers-in-law in the Sunnyside district, Al Knott and Jake Welty, fattened 700 lambs for the Chicago market. Over the next decade, Knott made sheep feeding his specialty. By the mid-1890s, sprawling corrals known as sheep pens could be found on nearly every farm in the Little Thompson Valley. Each fall farmers purchased lambs, fattened them with alfalfa over the winter, and shipped them to market in the spring.

Having established the valley's largest such operation on his farm northeast of town, Knott expanded by adding a mountain ranch near Corona on the top of Rollins Pass and a farm near Fort Morgan. Unlike many feeders, Knott held back part of his flock from market and sheared their wool. Each year he traveled as far as Mexico to purchase sheep for himself and other feeders.

In December 1898, the *Berthoud Bulletin* noted, "The following is a list of the persons who are feeding sheep in this vicinity and the number that is being fed by each: J.W. Shay, 1,216; W.T. Newell, 1,080; A.A. Knott, 4,000; D. Fagan, 1,125; G.F. Welty, 680; J.H. Welty, 340; W. Grip [*sic*], 788; F.M. Waggener, 2,050; E.H. Knott, 280; Munson and Gregg, 1,065; R.M. Hubbell, 1,480; W.R. Thornton, 1,080; O.J. Smith, 1,600 and J. Coleman, 300."

In 1900, a series of weak markets for sheep and wool forced Knott to withdraw from the sheep feeding business. Other Little Thompson Valley farmers continued on a lesser scale for several years.

Sheep being fattened for market at James Jensen's Sunnyslope Farm north of Berthoud, c. 1920. (Berthoud Historical Society)

Alvin T. Steinel, *History of Agriculture in Colorado*, The State Agricultural College, Fort Collins, Colorado, 1926, p. 150.

Frances Nielson, Helen Fickel, *The Heritage of Berthoud and the Little Thompson Valley*, Helen McCarty Fickel, Berthoud, Colorado, 1992.

Berthoud Bulletin, Dec. 15, 1898; July 3, 1952.

3.50   Women Enter Town Politics

In April 1894, one year after Colorado legalized full suffrage for women, Debbie Kelly and Jennie Jefferes won seats on Berthoud's town board. Kelly won her seat outright while Jefferes collected the same number of votes as Andrew Fairbairn. Lots were cast and Jefferes won the position. The women joined incumbents Charles M. Tilton, L. Van Delinder and William Clark, who was re-elected mayor. According to the *Fort Collins Courier*, every registered voter in Berthoud cast a ballot except Ella Bunyan, C.H. Welch and Griff Smith.

Debbie Huntsman Kelly, a former school teacher, was the wife of former Berthoud Postmaster and depot agent Leonard Kelly who had served on Berthoud's first town board in 1888. Jennie Buzzard Jefferes came to Berthoud in 1886 in a small party of covered wagons that camped across the road from Peter Turner's house. Her husband Sim Jefferes became one of the town's livery stable operators.

During their one-year terms, Kelly and Jefferes were members of a town board that approved a monthly salary of $37.50 for Town Marshal and Street & Water Commissioner Dan Osborn. That year the trustees also agreed to pay for a carpet to be installed in Berthoud's hose house. At that time the hose house was also used as Berthoud's jail and town hall.

Kelly and Jefferes also got entangled in a contentious dispute over saloons. In January 1895, Jefferes made headlines in the *Berthoud Bulletin* when it was revealed that she had discovered her husband had purchased whiskey for medical purposes at the Foresman & McCarty drugstore. When Jefferes reported the incident to a fellow trustee, the Board charged the drugstore with violating the town ordinance prohibiting the sales of intoxicating liquors.

Over the next few months, Berthoud's 300 citizens battled over whether the town should remain dry as it had been for the previous two years or become "wet" and allow saloons. On Election Day, Berthoud's "dry people" brought a Denver minister to town to campaign for their cause. After the votes were in and Berthoud remained dry, a gang of "wet folks" gathered a large supply of eggs and went looking for the minister. Unable to find him, they peppered a number of stores with "hen fruit."

In the municipal election held on April 2, 1895, incumbent mayor William Clark defeated Rev. W.H. McCormick by a margin of seven votes. A few days later new trustees Bill Forgy, Andrew Fairbairn, Ed Dudley and Alfred Bimson took office. It is not known if Kelly or Jefferes ran for re-election.

On May 14, 1895, a permit was granted to the Foresman & McCarty drugstore to sell liquor for medicinal purposes. Later that year, three private club rooms opened where members could drink liquor. This was in accordance with Berthoud's town ordinances.

Frances Nielson, Helen Fickel, *The Heritage of Berthoud and the Little Thompson Valley*, Helen McCarty Fickel, Berthoud, Colorado, 1992.

Belva Turner Bashor, *Early Berthoud: A History of the Town 1877-1900*, The Old Army Press, Fort Collins, Colorado, 1976, p. 64.

Berthoud Bulletin, Jan. 3, 1895.

Boulder Daily Camera, Apr. 4, 1895; June 29, 1895.

3.51 Handy Ditch War

In 1896, nearly two decades after the Handy Ditch Company was organized, a group of Berthoud farmers who felt they were being shortchanged by a Mr. Havener, the river commissioner, banded together to seize the water needed to save their parched crops. Water that Berthoud farmers considered theirs was being turned down the Big Thompson River to irrigate farms near Greeley.

Armed with rifles, a group of Handy stockholders including Frank Ricks, John C. Shull, Dick Hubbell, Ernest Newell, Henry Dunbar, Al Knott, Frank Knott, Willard Sanderson, Jim Lee, Luther Milburn, John McCormick and Herman Huppe rode to the Handy Dam at the mouth of the Big Thompson river canyon and opened the headgate, releasing water into the ditch that irrigated their farms near Berthoud.

When the Commissioner Havener got wind of their action, he dispatched his deputy, Vern Kempton, to the Handy Dam to close the headgate. J.C. Shull and another Berthoud man named Jennings met the deputy before he could act and explained their desperate plight. When the deputy said he had no choice but to shut off the water, Jennings pulled a pistol from his pocket and the other men, stationed on the cliff above, stepped into view with their rifles. The deputy withdrew.

Many year later one of the Berthoud men, Ernest Newell, wrote, "This went on for several days and they finally reached an agreement. It was an unfortunate occurrence for it did not settle anything."

Berthoud Bulletin, June 27, 1940; June 19, 1952.

3.52 New School in 1897

Prior to the 1896-97 school year, the District No. 13 school board determined that the schoolhouse built on the 500 block of 6th Street in 1887 was unstable and needed to be replaced. Even though the two-story building was brick, classes were dismissed on windy days because teachers feared the building would blow down.

In July 1896, contractor J.C. Working of Fort Collins was

awarded the contract to build a new schoolhouse in Berthoud at a cost of $4,800. The building was designed by well-known Fort Collins architect Montezuma Fuller. The site selected for the school, present-day Fickel Park, was a full city block bordered by Massachusetts and Mountain avenues on the north and south and 6th and 7th streets on the east and west.

Before the 1896-97 school year got underway, the local school board made arrangements to use the Bransom Building at 330 Massachusetts Avenue as a classroom for the primary department. Susie Turner, daughter of Berthoud town founder Peter Turner, was the teacher for 49 students in grades one, two and three. Recesses from class were held next door in the lot behind the Davis-Hartford Mercantile where the company stored farm implements.

The intermediate department was composed of 28 students in grades four through seven. The upper department included 25 students in grades eight, nine and ten. Classes for both departments were held in the Pinkley Building on Mountain

Berthoud School constructed in 1897. Photo c. 1900. (Berthoud Historical Society)

Avenue. Grace Shull, daughter of Berthoud businessman John C. Shull, taught both levels. "Professor" O.E. Jackson was the school's principal.

The crowded classrooms were breeding grounds for an epidemic of scarlet fever that closed the primary department in December 1896.

When classes resumed in January 1897, the new school was ready for occupancy. The two-story, red brick school building faced 6th Street and consisted of two large classrooms on each floor. A steam furnace was located in the basement. The principal's office shared the second floor. The original 1887 school house across the street to the east was torn down.

On June 2, 1898, the first commencement for students attending the new school took place at Tilton's Hall on East Mountain Avenue. That evening a capacity crowd witnessed Katie Fagan, Alice Brown and James Sybrandt Cole deliver graduation orations and receive diplomas from Professor Jackson.

In 1904, the school became overcrowded so a 24- by 30-foot frame building was erected where the town's first schoolhouse had once stood. The auxiliary schoolhouse was used for classes until 1908 when the 1897 building was doubled in size.

The school was enlarged by adding a four-room addition (a mirror image of the original structure) to the west side of the building. The project was completed by Berthoud contractor John A. Bell.

Berthoud Bulletin, Jan. 14, 1897; May 6, 1897; June 9, 1898; Sept. 16, 1899; Oct. 21, 1937.

Fort Collins Courier, July 9, 1896; July 30, 1896; Sept. 10, 1896; Dec. 3, 1896.

Frances Nielson, Helen Fickel, *The Heritage of Berthoud and the Little Thompson Valley*, Helen McCarty Fickel, Berthoud, Colorado, 1992.

3.53 Newspaper Rivalry

George W. Johnson was the former editor of the *Fort Morgan Herald*. He managed the Turner House in Berthoud after leasing the hotel from Peter Turner in 1895. His brother-in-law, Grant Halderman, had been the editor of the *Berthoud Bulletin* from April 1893 to October 1894.

Johnson's political views prompted him to begin publishing the *Berthoud News* in January 1897. At the time, J. Mack Mills was editor of the *Berthoud Bulletin*. Even though both men were Populists and members of the People's Party, they conducted lively political debates through their newspapers.

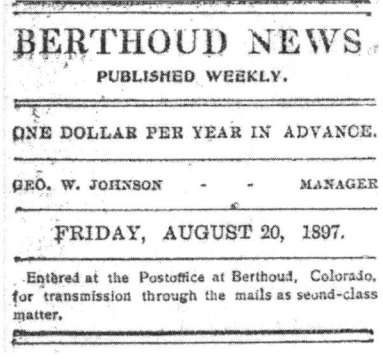

Berthoud News excerpt, Aug. 20, 1897.

Among the highly contentious issues of the day were the use of silver for coinage, women's rights and the prohibition of alcohol.

When Johnson began publishing the *Berthoud News* the *Fort Collins Express* commented, "Berthoud requires another newspaper about as bad as a wagon needs a fifth wheel."

Johnson operated the *Berthoud News* in an office on Mountain Avenue while Mills published the *Berthoud Bulletin* in a building east of the City Star Barn where he lived with his family. Mills was an attorney who also worked as a carpenter, photographer and music teacher, giving cornet and

Berthoud Bulletin advertisement in the *Directory of Weld and Larimer Counties, 1898.*

clarinet lessons during his residency in Berthoud from 1892 to 1898.

In 1897, J. Mack Mills was elected to the office of Larimer County judge. With his wife Belle he continued to publish the *Berthoud Bulletin* until May 1899 when he sold the newspaper to W.F. Phelps and relocated to Fort Collins. Mills became owner and editor of the *Fort Collins Review*, later trading that newspaper for a farm near Longmont.

George W. Johnson ceased publication of the *Berthoud News* in 1898 and moved to Longmont where he purchased the *Saturday Evening Call*. In 1905, he founded the *Daily Call* which he built into one of the state's finest small town newspapers.

Berthoud Bulletin, Jan. 21, 1897; Dec. 27, 1929; July 10, 1952.

Fort Collins Courier, Jan. 14, 1897.

Frances Nielson, Helen Fickel, *The Heritage of Berthoud and the Little Thompson Valley*, Helen McCarty Fickel, Berthoud, Colorado, 1992.

Berthoud News, Aug. 20, 1897.

3.54 Berthoud Business Enterprises — 1897

After J. Mack Mills became editor of the *Berthoud Bulletin* in January 1897, he strengthened ties with the community by publishing a series of articles promoting the town's businesses.

When Mills penned his articles in 1897, Berthoud had grown to nearly 300 residents. A bustling business district nearly filled the 500 block of 3rd Street as well as the 200 and 300 blocks of Mountain Avenue. The residential areas comprised two small neighborhoods, one that stretched a few blocks along Welch Avenue at the south edge of town, and another located north

and west of the business district. The majority of the community's populace, however, still lived in the agricultural districts
surrounding the town.

   Mills's first article profiled the Berthoud Roller Mills,
Berthoud Elevator Co. and C.M. Tilton Lumber & Coal Co.

1895 Sanborn map
of the Berthoud
Farmers Milling
& Elevator Co.
facility. (Berthoud
Historical Society)

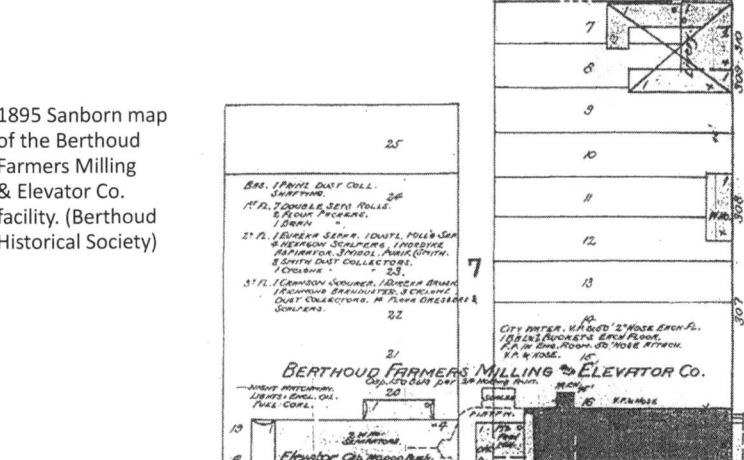

View of the Berthoud Elevator Co. buildings (center) looking south toward Mountain
Avenue, c. 1914. The Farmers Milling & Elevator Company's flour mill and the lumberyard may be seen at the left of the photo. (Berthoud Historical Society)

These enterprises occupied corners of the intersection of Mountain Avenue and the Union Pacific, Denver & Gulf railroad tracks, using rail sidings that flanked the east and west sides of the tracks.

Berthoud Roller Mills, also known as the Farmers' Milling & Elevator Company flour mill, consisted of a large grain elevator and flour mill at the northeast corner of the intersection. The mill could manufacture 175 barrels of flour every 24 hours. The company was the town's biggest employer and the largest buyer of grain in the area.

The Berthoud Elevator Co., owned by Denver mill magnate John K. Mullen, was located at the southwest corner of the intersection. The company stored grain in its Berthoud elevator until it could be shipped to Mullen's mill in Longmont, where it was ground into flour or livestock feed.

The southeast corner of the intersection was the site of the C.M. Tilton Lumber & Coal Company. The business occupied a two-story, frame building and several lumber and coal sheds. The second floor of the main building, Tilton's Hall, was also known to local residents as the Opera House.

Mills's second article promoted the One Price Cash Store, Berthoud Mercantile Co. and Golden Rule Store. The One Price

The C.M. Tilton Lumber & Coal Co. building in 1897, later sold to the Peter Mintener Lumber Co. c. 1920. (Berthoud Historical Society)

Davis, Brown & McAllaster Store, c. 1914. (Berthoud Historical Society)

Cash Store, operated by Duncan May and Charles Pollock, was located in the two-story brick building at the southwest corner of 3rd Street and Massachusetts Avenue, featuring general merchandise ranging from graniteware to children's shoes. William Flora ran a meat market next door in a building that had been moved from Old Berthoud to the new town in 1884.

The Berthoud Mercantile Co. was operated by Daniel Mahan while the Berthoud Golden Rule Store was managed by Mrs. E.J. Fenters. Fenters's business was one of several Golden Rule stores in Northern Colorado. Both stores were located in the 500 block of 3rd Street.

Mills's third installment of "Berthoud Enterprises" plugged the Davis-Hartford Mercantile Company. Located at the northwest corner of 3rd Street and Massachusetts Avenue, Davis-Hartford was the oldest hardware and farm implement dealer in town. Established in 1886, destroyed by a blaze in 1888, and rebuilt on a larger scale later that year, Davis-Hartford offered everything needed from the "cradle to the grave." Arthur F. Brown, in charge of farm implement sales in 1897, eventually became a partner in the business.

The Davis-Hartford company's main competition was the W.H. McCormick Implement Emporium at the corner of 3rd

Street and Mountain Avenue, housed in an L-shaped building that wrapped around the Bank of Berthoud. A former pastor and Larimer County Representative to the Colorado Legislature, McCormick later expanded his inventory and advertised that "McCormick Sells Everything!"

The McCormick store located "next door" on either side of the Bank of Berthoud in 1897, c. December 1913. (Berthoud Historical Society)

In his fourth article, Mills profiled the town's doctors and drugstores. Dr. William W. Cole, the first physician to establish a medical practice in Berthoud, was based in a building two doors south of May & Pollock's One Price Cash Store. President William McKinley's administration appointed Cole as postmaster in 1897. Cole located the town's post office in his drugstore.

The Foresman & McCarty Drugstore, operated by pharmacist Harley Foresman and physician David W. McCarty, was also located in the 500 block of 3rd Street. McCarty maintained his practice in rooms at the rear of the drugstore but also made house calls in a horse and buggy he kept on call at the City Star Barn.

Two of Berthoud's blacksmiths, Alfred Bimson and Pappy Fenton, and a wagon maker, Sam D. Lutener, were the topic of a subsequent article in the *Bulletin*. Before the Panic of 1893, Bimson had five forges in operation. When Mills wrote his articles in 1897, Bimson's business was rebounding, and he was teaching the trade to his brother-in-law, Henry Eichman.

In 1897, Pappy Fenton was back to work as a blacksmith in his shop at the northeast corner of 4th Street and Mountain Avenue. Before the town was moved from the river bottom, Fenton had operated a forge at Old Berthoud. He left the trade to take a job at the flour mill in the new town, but his position was eliminated during the Panic. Mills noted, "Pap is getting pretty well along in years but he can hit as hard and make the sparks fly as far as any of them."

The town's wagon maker, Sam Lutener, operated his business in a shop at the northeast corner of 2nd Street and Mountain Avenue. His brother, John M. Lutener, also ran a carpentry and painting business from the same building.

Mills publicized Berthoud's two livery stables in his seventh article. The City Stables, owned by Lew Hertha, occupied a site on East Mountain Avenue, east of the C.M. Tilton Lumber & Coal Company. The City Star Barn, operated by Sim Jefferes,

Alfred Bimson's stone blacksmith shop, constructed by stonemason J.C. Lurvey in 1893. (Berthoud Historical Society)

was located one block west of Hertha on Mountain Avenue. In addition to hauling freight, renting buggies and selling coal, Jefferes sold flour and feed for the Berthoud Elevator Co.

The short-lived Berthoud Creamery, located on the north side of the 200 block of East Mountain Avenue, was the subject of Mills's eighth article. Established in 1896, the business was a branch of the Longmont Creamery Company. After cream was separated from milk at the Berthoud plant, it was shipped to Longmont where it was processed into buttermilk, butter, sweet milk, skim milk, and cottage cheese.

Mills profiled several Berthoud tradesmen in his ninth article. Daniel Overacker, a cobbler who did not have the use of his legs, ran a shoe shop in a small frame building at the southwest corner of 3rd Street and Mountain Avenue. Overacker's wife wheeled him to work until blacksmith Alfred Bimson built a tricycle that enabled Overacker to propel the contraption with hand levers. A Mr. Langley also had a shoemaking shop next door to W.H. McCormick's Implement Emporium.

Lew Hertha's City Stables, c. 1907. (Berthoud Historical Society)

Henry Corcoran made his living plastering houses and constructing cisterns. S. Fremont Curtis and Warren L. Mills, the father of *Berthoud Bulletin* editor J. Mack Mills, were among the town's house builders. Berthoud's stonemasons, B.O. Hendron and John Lurvey, laid foundations and sidewalks. Lurvey's stone quarry was located in the foothills west of Berthoud.

S.F. Curtis (left) was among Berthoud's house builders in 1897. (Berthoud Historical Society)

Mills concluded his series of articles with endorsements of the Berthoud Produce Company, Atwood's Jewelry Store and Beal's Harness Shop. The Berthoud Produce Company, located in a large warehouse near the train depot, sat on a rail siding where locally grown produce could be loaded into boxcars and shipped to outside markets. The business also sold seed grain and seed potatoes. Al Atwood, the jeweler in 1896, moved from the Foresman & McCarty drugstore into the building that was also occupied by the Bank of Berthoud. John Beal, the harness maker, came to Berthoud in 1895. Shortly after his arrival, Beal constructed a brick business building at 343 Mountain Avenue. In addition to harnesses, Beal sold a line of veterinary supplies and bicycles.

Berthoud Bulletin, Jan. 28, 1897; Feb. 4, 1897; Feb. 18, 1897; Feb. 25, 1897; Mar. 4, 1897; Mar. 11, 1897; Mar. 18, 1897; Mar. 25, 1897; Apr. 1, 1897; Apr. 22, 1897.

3.55 Berthoud Wheel Club

When owning a "wheel" became the rage in Berthoud in the late 1890s, several businessmen began selling bicycles. One was John Beal who sold and repaired bicycles at his harness shop. John Bunyan also sold a line of Rambler bicycles from his office at the Bank of Berthoud. The Davis-Hartford Mercantile stocked bicycles that sold for nearly $100 each.

In May 1897, the *Berthoud Bulletin* announced that everyone who rode bicycles was invited to meet at the hose house to organize a "wheel club." On Friday, May 14, 1897, the club was formed and F. Irving Davis, Thomas Bunyan, Charles Pollock and Amos Mahan were elected president, secretary, captain and lieutenant, respectively. Pollock was charged with supervising "runs and excursions." The following evening, 18 bicyclists tooted tin horns and clanked cowbells as they paraded through the streets of Berthoud to celebrate the creation of their new club.

Ramblers.............$80
Ideals..........$35 to $75
1 Cleveland, (²d hand).....$40
John Bunyan.

John Bunyan, whose father operated the Bank of Berthoud, sold new and used bicycles in 1897. (*Berthoud Bulletin*, May 6, 1897)

No further news about the Berthoud Wheel Club appeared in the *Bulletin*. The tabloid did, however, report that local residents, including Sid Davis and James Vigar, had ridden their "wheels" to Longmont and Greeley.

By 1899, it was apparent that "wheels" were a problem on Berthoud's sidewalks. In June of that year, one of Walter Greenland's boys was riding his bicycle on the

sidewalk in front of Lew Hertha's livery stable when he col-
lided with a horse. He avoided serious injury, but the incident
prompted the town board, later that month, to pass an ordinance prohibiting bicycles on sidewalks.

Berthoud Bulletin, May 13, 1897; May 20, 1897; Apr. 21, 1898; June 12, 1899.

3.56 Beginning of the Sugar Beet Industry

The local sugar beet industry came to life in January 1898 when
a mass meeting was held at Tilton's Hall to discuss the possibility of building a sugar factory in Berthoud. It was rumored
that a group of Eastern capitalists were seeking a location in
Northern Colorado to build a sugar factory. Lumberyard owner
C.M. Tilton and banker Thomas C. Bunyan were chosen to go to
Denver to investigate. Similar committees were formed in the
nearby communities of Loveland and Fort Collins.

Sugar beets, the cash crop that would be king of Northern

Berthoud beet dump, c. 1910. (Berthoud Historical Society)

Colorado for many years, were introduced to the Berthoud area in the spring of 1898 when free seed was offered to farmers. Representatives of the Colorado Agricultural College in Fort Collins distributed the seed and growing instructions at the C.M. Tilton Lumber & Coal Co.

J. Mack Mills, editor of the *Bulletin*, mocked the prospect of a sugar factory in Berthoud as "air castles." However, George Johnson of the *Berthoud News* backed the effort and worked to secure a factory.

Mills skewered his rival by writing, "The people of this community are anxious for a sugar beet factory and there is no question about their ability and willingness to furnish all the beets that an institution of this kind could work, providing the sugar trust wouldn't insist on hogging all the profits as similar institutions have been in the habit of doing with other products of the farm. They are not, however, pining for a sugar factory as has often appeared in print the last week or two. Manufactured beets won't go. Those fellows who are trying to saddle a sugar beet or any other kind of 'beat' factory on this community will find they will have an uphill pull. Our farmers will insist on raising beets whether they be sugar beets or dead beats—it has been fully demonstrated that we can produce our share of either."

In a subsequent issue of the *Bulletin* Mills added, "WANTED: A few pairs of jackass ears. There are some people in this community who need them in order to look like they act."

In the spring of 1899, debate over the construction of a sugar factory shifted to Loveland where greater effort had been invested to bring the industry to that town. While various Berthoud business owners and beet growers still wanted a factory built in Berthoud, they all backed the construction of such a facility in Loveland where beets grown on Berthoud farms could be processed.

In the early 1900s, sugar beets became the cornerstone of Northern Colorado's agricultural economy. In 1906, another effort was mounted to convince the Great Western Sugar Company to build a factory on a site south of Berthoud owned by Charles C. Welch. That prospect did not materialize even though the Little Thompson Valley surrounding Berthoud had earned a reputation as one of the region's best beet-growing areas.

Berthoud Bulletin, Jan. 6, 1898; Jan. 27, 1898; Feb. 3, 1898; Apr. 7, 1898; May 19, 1898; May 11, 1899; May 18, 1899; July 14, 1906.

Fort Collins Courier, Feb. 17, 1898.

3.57 Berthoud Up-to-Date

In March 1899, Berthoud's leaders felt so confident in the town's ability to attract prospective residents that the *Bulletin* dedicated one full page to the promotion of the community. Sketches of prominent business owners were interspersed with descriptions of the town's churches, schools, bank, newspaper and hotel. The purpose was to attract potential citizens includ-

Looking north from Mountain Avenue at the 500 block of 3rd Street, c. 1905. (Berthoud Historical Society)

ing "...farmers, stock-raisers and others who are looking for a safe place for sound investments."

According to the *Bulletin*, Berthoud's municipal government was "...based on strict ideas of economy, consistent with safe and secure progress." Alfred Bimson was the town's mayor and John Lutener, George Davis, Sim Jefferes, Sam Lutener,

Among Berthoud's up-and-coming young men of the late 1890s were (back row left to right) S. Ernest Newell, Ben Sexton, (front row) unidentified, Harry Newell, and Hank Lovejoy. (Berthoud Historical Society)

Wilbur Thornton and Harry Lovejoy were the councilmen. J. Mack Mills had relocated to Fort Collins but was still employed as the town's attorney. The newspaper praised the town's populace as "...essentially a church-going people" and identified the community's places of worship including the United Brethren, Presbyterian and Christian churches.

The Berthoud School was described as "A-1 in every particular" and the Bank of Berthoud was declared as safe as any similar institution in Colorado. The town had a weekly newspaper, the *Berthoud Bulletin*, and the Grandview Hotel provided "...first-class accommodations to transient and permanent guests."

The tabloid also identified the Masons, Independent Order of Odd Fellows, Knights of Pythias, Woodmen of the World and the Daughters of Rebecca as the town's "secret orders." There was mention of the brass band and fire company, both financed by public subscription.

In a pitch to prospective businessmen, the newspaper added, "...the surrounding country for a radius of many miles is practically tributary to this place in most of its lines of trade." The Union Pacific Railroad (successor to the Colorado Central), which intersected Berthoud and the Little Thompson Valley, was commended for reasonable rates, making it possible to profitably ship freight and livestock.

Berthoud Bulletin, Mar. 2, 1899.

Afterword

As the 1890s drew to a close, the relocation of the town from the river bottom to the bluff had proven to be a success. Berthoud was ready to boom as the agricultural center of southern Larimer County.

Berthoud's growth had been hindered by a housing shortage ever since its relocation from the Little Thompson river bottom in the winter of 1883-84. The early 1900s saw Berthoud's population expand when real estate developers and contractors built houses and the two-story, red brick "business blocks" that became prominent symbols of the town's potential prosperity.

The Great Western Sugar Company established itself in Northern Colorado in the early 1900s. The company constructed several sugar factories including plants at Loveland and Longmont where beets grown in Berthoud's rural districts were shipped for processing. Raising sugar beets required a larger labor force so the company brought seasonal workers to the area, a large number of whom remained to help build the community as permanent residents.

The era of the wagon trails and hardscrabble homesteaders faded from memory as Berthoud embarked on a future promising all the modern conveniences of 20th century life. Memories of Berthoud's early days were left on the river bottom as the town settled in on the bluff.

Acknowledgments

I wish to thank the Berthoud Historical Society, an organization dedicated to preserving the heritage of Berthoud and the Little Thompson Valley, for providing many of the images used in this book. I also thank Bill Meirath who helped establish a context for the Cherokee Trail by making available to me the rare John Carbutt stereoscopic view of Mariano Medina at "Bear's Cathedral near the Big Thompson."

I extend my gratitude to John Meissner who opened doors to newspaper archives that otherwise would have been overlooked; Mary Edelmaier and Mark Wolenetz who proofread the first manuscripts; Sarah Donohoe whose editing elevated the book's content to a higher level; and LaVonne Ewing and Diane Streb who expertly designed the book.

I am most indebted to Larimer County historian Kenneth Jessen whose encouragement and willingness to share his professional network motivated and enabled me to chronicle the early years of the Little Thompson Valley and the transition of Berthoud, Colorado, from the river bottom to the bluff.

Index

Crane, Frank, 118, 130, 133, 135, 140, 146, 159-162, 209-210
Cresswell, David F., 212-213
Cronk, George, 53, 62
Cross, Ida, 129
Cross, Lewis, 44, 47, 53, 57-63, 66, 71-73, 83, 86-87, 94, 97, 99-102, 111-112, 117-118. 120, 129, 131
Crossville, 86
Culver, Cary, 44-52, 64, 74
Culver School, 65
Cunningham, J.M., 68
Curtis, S.F., 237

Dapp, David, 101
Daughters of Rebecca, 243
Davis & Hartford, 150-151, 163-164, 173, 206, 216, 227, 233
Davis, Franklin Irving, 128, 150, 155, 161-169, 181, 187, 211, 219, 238
Davis, George, 243
Davis, Ida, 166
Davis, Imogene, 166
Davis, James, 187, 194
Davis, Nettie, 166, 208
Davis, Sidney. 166, 238
Davis, W.H., 107
Day, Edward, 101
Day, John, 143
DeFrance, Judge Allison H., 94, 178
Dennis, H.P., 217
Denver Pacific Railroad & Telegraph Co., 142
depot, 135-137
Derby, Will, 193
Dewey, Joseph, 211
Dix, Ben, 184
Dixon Hill, 215
Dobbins, Sam, 144, 189
Dolloff & Dycer, 151
Dolloff, J.W., 147, 180-181
Donovan Bros., 164
Dry Creek Lateral Ditch, 96

Dudley, Ed, 225
Dunbar, Henry, 226
Dunraven, Lord, 189
Dycer, William, 151

Eaglin, James, 45-46, 52, 54, 61-62, 74
Edmondson Company (Cherokee Trail), 20-22, 24, 30
Eichman, Henry, 235
Eldora, 195

electricity, 216
Ellermeyer, E.W., 194
Emrick, J.A., 84
Engels Company (Cherokee Trail), 22
Estes Park, 189
Evans Company (Cherokee Trail), 19
Everhard, John B., 78
Everhard, John W., 72, 74, 76-78, 88, 97-98. 101, 107, 120, 129, 138, 161
Everitt, F.E., 94

Fagan, Daniel, 223
Fagan, Jennie, 203
Fagan, Katie, 228
Fairbairn & Hankins, 181
Fairbairn, Andrew, 141, 151, 162, 168-169, 181-182, 193-194, 205, 224-225
Fairbairn Davis Lumber & Coal Co., 151, 216
Fairbairn's Hall, 180-181, 200
Fairman, Annie, 67
Farmers Milling & Elevator Co., 118, 158-159, 168, 179-181, 189, 209, 232
Farwell, Cyrus, 101
Fenters, Mrs. E.J., 233
Fenton, Frank, 143
Fenton, Isa, 156
Fenton, Walter (Pappy), 107, 112, 118, 131-132, 200, 234
Fenton, William, 143, 211
Ferguson, Anna, 188
Ferguson & Hallett Ranch, 153

List of Maps

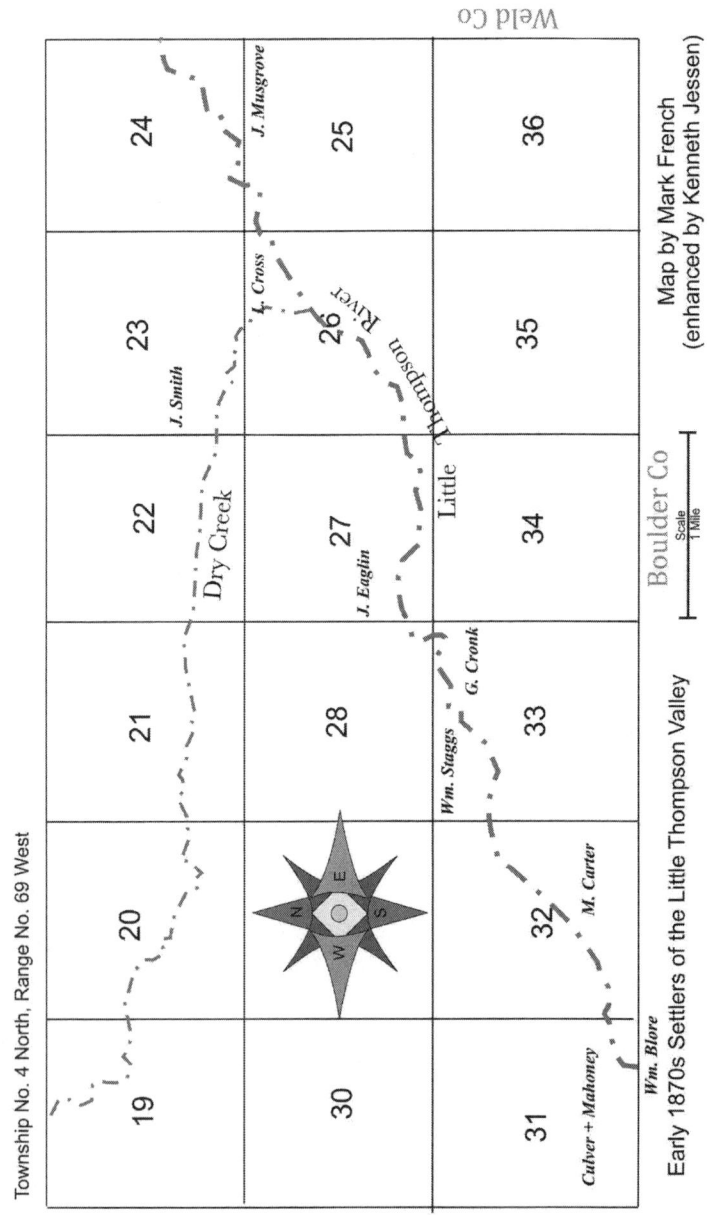

Land lying along the Little Thompson river bottom was the first to be claimed in the early 1870s. (Mark French and Kenneth Jessen map)

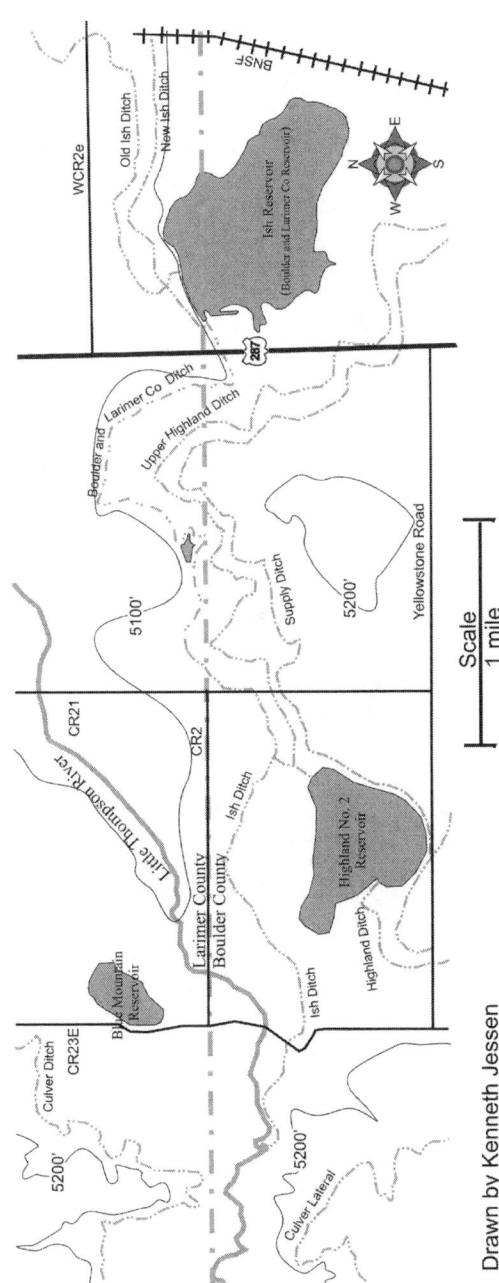

The ditch and reservoir of the Boulder and Larimer County Irrigating and Manufacturing Company is located on the southern slopes of the Little Thompson Valley south of present-day Berthoud.

Drawn by Kenneth Jessen

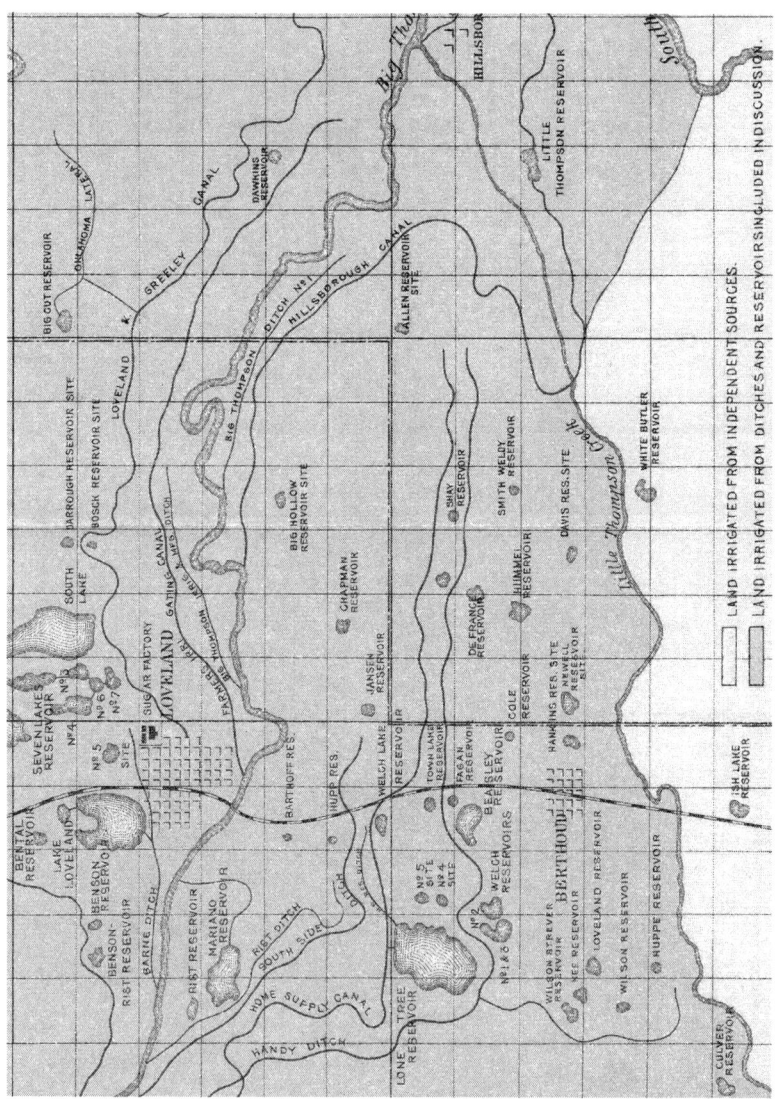

Handy Ditch and other southern Larimer County ditches and irrigation reservoirs. (U.S. Dept. of Agriculture, 1901) Note the names of many early settlers attached to various reservoirs: Culver, Ish, Huppe, Wilson, Loveland, Welch, Davis, Hummel, DeFrance, Hankins, Newell, Smith, etc.

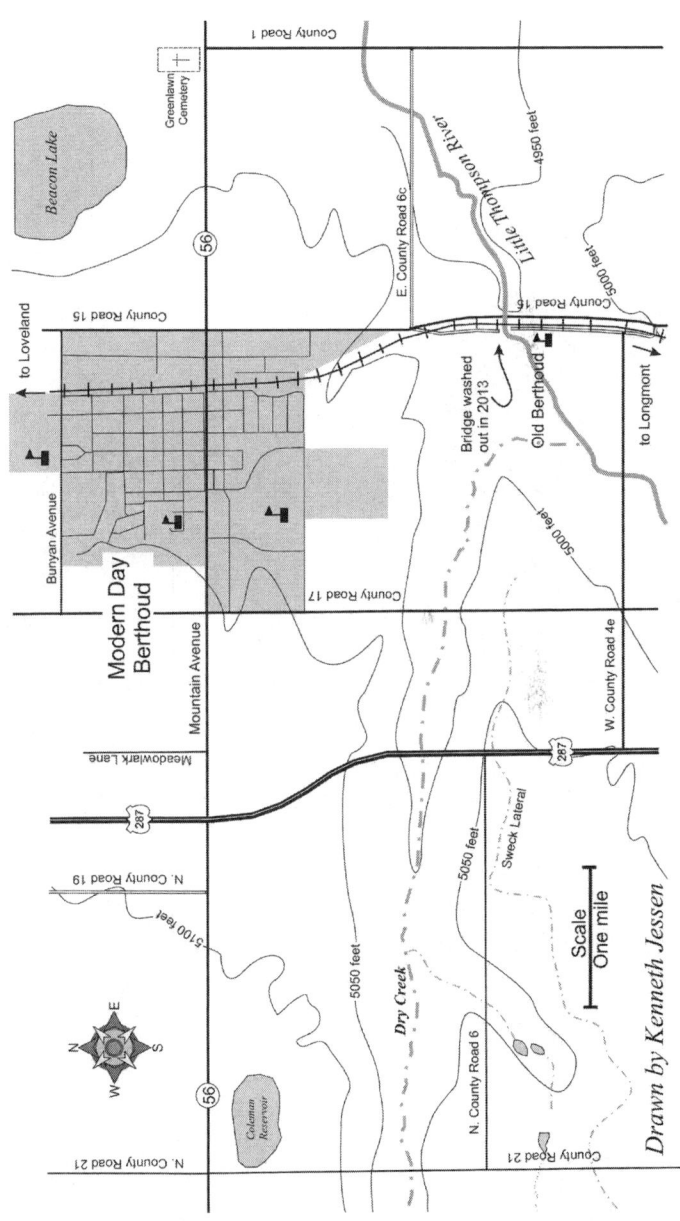

The original Berthoud settlement, identified as "Old Berthoud" was moved to "Modern Day Berthoud" in the winter of 1883-84. (Map by Kenneth Jessen)

Author Mark French

 A fifth-generation Coloradoan, Mark French became interested in local history when his junior high school teacher assigned an independent research project. French selected the far-too-broad topic of Berthoud's history and while rifling through stacks of bound copies of old *Berthoud Bulletin* newspapers thought, "Someone should have written a book about this." Now French has.

Since those days French has penned over 900 articles on the history of Berthoud and the surrounding Little Thompson Valley of north central Colorado. This book, the result of several years of research, uncovers the early history of French's native stomping grounds.

Mark French is a lifetime member of the Berthoud Historical Society and has served as its president since 2000. He is a charter member of Historic Larimer County and also belongs to the Colorado Cherokee Chapter of the Oregon-California Trails Association (OCTA).

Made in the USA
Columbia, SC
27 June 2022